The Beast that Crouches at the Door

Adam & Eve, Cain & Abel, and Beyond

A Biblical Exploration by
Rabbi David Fohrman

DEVORA
PUBLISHING
JERUSALEM ◆ NEW YORK

The author invites feedback.
He can be contacted at:
davidfohrman@gmail.com.

The Beast that Crouches at the Door
Published by Devora Publishing Company
Text Copyright © 2007 by Hoffberger Foundation for Torah Studies, a
support foundation of the Associated Jewish Community Federation of
Baltimore

First impression 2007
Second impression 2008

COVER DESIGN: Michelle Levy, Jerusalem Typesetting
TYPESETTING & BOOK DESIGN: Raphaël Freeman, Jerusalem Typesetting
EDITOR: Carol Selkin Wise
EDITORIAL & PRODUCTION MANAGER: Daniella Barak

Hard Cover ISBN: 978-1-932687-79-3

E-MAIL: sales@devorapublishing.com
WEB SITE: www.devorapublishing.com

Printed in the United States of America.

ৡ Contents

PART II: THE WORLD'S FIRST MURDER:
A CLOSER LOOK AT CAIN AND ABEL

‫ Acknowledgments

This book had its beginnings on a cold winter's night about ten years ago, in the parking lot of Johns Hopkins University, just outside Shaffer Hall.

I had been teaching a class on the Book of Genesis. That night we had been talking about Adam and Eve in the Garden of Eden, and a group of students stayed afterwards to continue the discussion. Two of them – LeRoy Hoffberger and his wife, Rebecca – stayed longer than the others, and walked me to my car. In the Never-Never Land somewhere between my car and theirs, we lost ourselves probing the implications of this mysterious story. Bundled up against the cold, our conversation lasted well into the night.

That conversation was the beginning of a long friendship between the Hoffbergers and me. LeRoy and Rebecca cared deeply about the underlying meaning of this story, and more generally, about how knowledge of Torah could and should inform one's life. LeRoy envisioned creating an institute devoted to the kind of Torah study we had been doing in our class at Johns Hopkins – and over time, he brought this vision to fruition. LeRoy founded the

Hoffberger Foundation for Torah Studies, and asked me to serve as its resident scholar.

Teaching Biblical themes had always been a passion of mine, but I never thought I would be lucky enough to devote my professional life to this dream. The Hoffbergers have made that intense desire a reality for me. Through their efforts, a conversation in a parking lot has blossomed into countless classes – and now, at long last, a book. Along the way, they have become close friends, devoted students, constructive critics – and surrogate grandparents to our kids. Gratitude is perhaps too pedestrian a word to express my feelings towards LeRoy and Rebecca. But maybe it's a start. I am deeply privileged to call them partners in my life's work.

Although LeRoy has been the driving force behind the foundation, he has not been alone in pursuing its aims. He and I would like to express gratitude to its other principal funders, including the Harry and Jeanette Weinberg Foundation, the Hoffberger Family Foundation, and The Associated: Jewish Community Federation of Baltimore.

There were many others who participated in the process of bringing this book from the realm of vision into reality. They include Yaacov Peterseil, publisher at Devora Publishing, who early on saw merit in the manuscript, worked to procure it, and ably set about the process of bringing the book to fruition. Carol Wise skillfully edited the manuscript, and Azriella Jaffe, herself an accomplished author, reviewed the entire book and made innumerable meaningful suggestions. Daniella Barak capably managed the production process.

A book begins long before an author writes down what is on his mind. Before that, he has to actually *have* something on his mind. In that spirit, I want to acknowledge those who, over the years, helped shape my way of thinking, and guide my development as a student of Torah.

The person who perhaps most profoundly influenced my life and way of thinking was my late father, Moshe Fohrman, *zt"l*. He died before I became a *Bar Mitzvah*, but in those early years,

ACKNOWLEDGMENTS

taught me much of what I know about what makes life worthwhile, and how to practice the art of living in a meaningful way.
He was not a scholar in the technical sense of the word, but he
was one of the wisest persons I have been privileged to know. I
hope that he would regard this book as a worthy expression of
his spiritual legacy.

As I was growing up, I was lucky to be exposed to Rabbi
Yosef Leibowitz, who now lives in Kfar Saba, Israel, but then was
the rabbi of the *shul* in the San Francisco Bay Area to which our
family belonged. I was fascinated by the way he read Biblical text,
and found myself captivated by his sermons. I can still remember our preparing my Bar Mitzvah speech together. He asked me
to read the Torah portion on my own, and to come back to him
with questions about it that were of greatest concern to me. With
these questions in the background, the words of the ancient commentators somehow seemed to jump off the page and brim with
life. The whole process made *me* feel alive, and gave me a taste of
a kind of learning I knew I would want to try and pursue.

I spent many years studying at the Ner Israel Rabbinical
College, and I feel honored to count the Rosh Yeshiva of that
institution, the late Rav Yaakov Weinberg *zt"l*, as a mentor. As a
young high school student, I didn't know you weren't supposed to
call the Rosh Yeshiva up on the dorm phone to ask if you could
drop by his home and chat about some questions. Somehow, that
approach didn't display the proper degree of reverence. But he
graciously extended himself to me, and I was very fortunate to
benefit from years of his guidance, wisdom and concern. Other
faculty members at Ner Israel – including Rabbis Tzvi Berkowitz,
Moshe Eisemann and Nachum Lansky – introduced new vistas
of thinking to me. And weekly *hashkafa chaburos* – sessions in
Jewish Philosophy – given by Rabbi Ezra Neuberger, grounded
me in oft-overlooked "basics" of Jewish thought, and opened my
mind to possibilities I found both tantalizing and profoundly
meaningful.

While at Ner Israel, I benefited from an enduring relationship with Rabbi Hermann Neuberger, who – it sounds like a cliché but it's true – was really like a father to me. I was often a guest at his home for *Shabbos* meals, and found myself intrigued by the conversation and inspired by his persona. I am profoundly thankful for the strong interest he took throughout the years in my personal development and welfare, and for his wise counsel, of which I availed myself frequently. I count myself fortunate in that I came to know not just him, but virtually all of his children as well. R' Sheftel, R' Shraga, R' Yaakov, and R' Ezra each opened their homes and hearts to me, and were mentors to me in their own right.

In later years, I came to treasure a friendship with Rabbi Yehezkel Danziger, editor in chief of ArtScroll's Schottenstein Edition of the Talmud. The observations he shared with me about life and Torah are precious – but besides that, he taught me much of what I know about writing with concision, precision and care. His ability to express complex ideas with elegance and simplicity is something I admire and seek to emulate.

Throughout the years, my mother has been a beacon of love and compassion, and an emotional bulwark of support to me and to the rest of our family. All mothers strive to do this, I suppose – but she has done it exceedingly well. When she married my stepfather, Mr. Zev Wolfson, she brought into my life a man who has come to share her intense interest in my welfare and development. Over the years, he has guided my growth as a Jew and as a person, and I deeply cherish his love for me. For the last ten years or so, we have been *chevrusas*, study partners, together – sometimes in person, and sometimes by phone – and this has brought another, added, dimension to our relationship. I am proud to have become part of his family.

My wife Reena has been simultaneously my greatest fan and most incisive critic. If I can convince her of the merit of an idea, then I can convince anybody. Her loving attention to our children has helped us raise six wonderful kids. Her love for me and belief in my work have given me the strength and emotional sustenance to go forward in life. I am privileged to have her as my life's partner, and hope and pray we shall celebrate many more milestones together.

Part I

Serpents of Desire:
Good and Evil in the Garden of Eden

ℰ Introduction

Beyond the Lullaby Effect: Reading the Bible with Open Eyes

Paradoxically enough, a great problem that faces us when we study the Torah is that its stories are so familiar to us. No matter where you grew up, no matter what level of education you've had, you've come across the story of Adam and Eve tens, if not hundreds, of times. We've heard the story in school, and we've learned it at home. We drink Adam and Eve apple juice and see Adam and Eve icons repeatedly in advertising. We *know* that story, we assure ourselves. Indeed, we know the story too well for our own good.

When we know a story too well, we become easy prey to a syndrome I like to call the Lullaby Effect. The Lullaby Effect blocks our ability to ask, or even to see, the really important questions that the Bible begs us to ask of it. The Lullaby Effect anesthetizes us through the stupefying effects of familiarity.

Here's how it works. When was the last time you bothered thinking about the words of the lullabies you've known since

1

childhood? Stop for a moment and think – really think – about what their words actually mean. For starters, try that perennial favorite, "Rock-a-bye baby on the treetop." Imagine your child were actually paying attention to the words you were singing: "… when the bough breaks, the cradle will fall, and down will come baby, cradle and all."

Now, you can certainly get a kid to sleep by singing this. But if your sweet child were actually listening to what you were singing, she'd be in for a rude awakening. Lots of questions, I imagine, would quickly come to mind. If *we* bothered listening, they would come to our mind, too. "Exactly how far off the ground was the cradle when it fell?" "Did anyone call 911?" "Who put the cradle on the bough in the first place?" "Was the parent trying to get rid of the child?" "Are *you* trying to get rid of *me*?"

But no one asks these questions. Few of us are even remotely disturbed by the violence we sing about when trying to get our children to sleep. Why? Because we've simply stopped listening to the words. We have heard them too many times. We heard them as children before we even knew what they meant; and now, even as adults, they fail to shock us.

Biblical stories are a lot like lullabies in that way. Almost every major story in the Torah has its "elephant in the room" – some major problem, or a series of them, that cries out to be addressed. Why would God tell Abraham to take his son and kill him, only to retract at the last moment and say He didn't really mean it? What, exactly, did God have against the building of a tower in the Land of Babel? Why would God bother bargaining with Pharaoh to let the Jews go, only to harden his heart once the Egyptian monarch finally agreed? But the stories are too familiar to us. We've heard about them so many times, they've become part of our cultural fabric. We absorb the stories through osmosis, the way we unthinkingly develop accents that reflect the place where we grew up. We fail to see the problems anymore.

In this book, I'm going to challenge you to change all that. Come along with me on a journey, an adventure through biblical

2

text. Let's read these stories that we thought we knew with fresh eyes and ask the questions that any intelligent reader would ask about them.

If this idea makes you nervous, relax. We needn't fear these questions, for they are not really problems; they are opportunities. They are windows that the text gives us to perceive its deeper meaning. Sure, you can keep the window closed and pretend it isn't there. But if you don't open it, the treasure that lies beyond – a richer, three-dimensional understanding of the Torah, not to mention the entire world of rabbinic literature – will remain sealed off to you forever.

So here's the deal: before you go any further, I invite you first of all to re-read the story of Adam, Eve, and the serpent in the Garden of Eden. If you know Hebrew, read it in Hebrew; and if you don't, read it in translation. For the time being, any translation will do. Yes, I know, you *know* the story already – ever since sixth grade, you've had this image in your mind of the snake wound around the tree, offering Eve an apple. But that's precisely the point. You need to forget all that. You need to erase those images and read the story anew. You need to break the Lullaby Effect.

Read the story slowly and carefully. Just the text; no commentaries. And as you do, ask yourself these questions: If I were reading this for the first time, what about it would strike me as strange? What are the "big questions" that the Torah wants me to ask about this story? What are the elephants in the room? Take some time to think about it. I'll meet you right back here and we'll compare notes.

See you then.

Adam, Eve, and the Elephant in the Room

Okay, let's say you've taken some time to re-read the story of Adam, Eve, and the snake. (If you haven't, you can read my short summary below.) Hopefully, you've read it with fresh eyes and asked yourself that very basic of questions: "What is strange about this picture?" Before getting to your conclusions, let's take a moment to revisit the basic storyline together. In a nutshell, here it is:

> After creating a world, God fashions two human beings and places them in Paradise, the Garden of Eden. God gives them virtually free reign over the territory. There's only one restriction: a certain tree is off-limits – the tree labeled "the Tree of Knowledge of Good and Evil." The fruit of this tree must not be eaten under any circumstances.
>
> It doesn't take long for the human beings to transgress the only prohibition given to them. At the behest of a mysterious snake, Eve eats from the tree and shares the fruit with Adam. The Almighty becomes angry and hands out various

punishments: the snake? No more walking upright for him; he must crawl on his belly and eat dust. The woman? Generations of her kind will endure pain in conception and childbirth. And the man? He and his progeny will have to work by the sweat of their brow to make bread. And just to round things out, death is meted out to all the parties; nobody gets to live forever anymore.

Moreover, Eden is placed off-limits; everyone has to find somewhere else to live now. The great Lifeguard in the Sky has blown His whistle and it's time for everybody to get out of the pool. Why? Because there's another mysterious tree in the Garden – the Tree of Life – and the last thing God wants is anyone eating anything from *that* tree.

Well, what are the issues here? Does the story sit well with you, or do you find yourself uneasy with it? If you *are* uneasy, can you identify exactly *why* you are uneasy?

As I mentioned earlier, many biblical stories have their "elephant in the room," an obvious, deeply troubling, "why-didn't-I-think-of-that" question at the heart of the story. Is there a question of this sort, a question of this magnitude, that we need to address when reading the story of Adam and Eve in the Garden of Eden? I think there is.

Let's talk a little bit about this mysterious tree in the Garden, the one that God places off-limits. It has a name. It is known as the Tree of Knowledge of Good and Evil. By any measure, that's a pretty strange name for a tree, but if that's what the Bible calls it, then that's presumably what it is. It somehow conveys a knowledge of good and evil, an ability to distinguish right from wrong, to those who partake of its fruits.

But there's a big problem with this. Why would God want to deny this knowledge to people? Think about it. Are human beings better or worse off for their knowledge of good and evil? Is knowing right from wrong an asset or a liability for humanity? Imagine a world in which people are pretty much the same as they are now. They are smart; they can walk; they can talk; they can drive cars and become investment bankers. They are missing only one thing. They don't know right from wrong. We have a word for people like this. We call them sociopaths.

A person with all the faculties we associate with humanity except for the capacity to understand right and wrong is someone who could slaughter people with an axe the way you and I mow the lawn. Did God really want to create a society filled with such people? Clearly, people are better off when they know the difference between right and wrong. So why would God want to withhold this knowledge?

A tempting way out of the dilemma would be to suggest that somehow it was all a set-up. God really *did* want people to have the knowledge the tree would give them and was in fact glad when they ate from it. But this approach is deeply problematic. For the way the Torah tells the story, the Almighty seems pretty disappointed with Adam and Eve when they eat from the tree. In fact, He punishes them severely. How are we to understand this disappointment? It seems rather perverse to imagine the Almighty secretly chuckling with pleasure that Adam and Eve finally ate the fruit He put off limits while hiding this joy behind a mask of displeasure and anger.

Clearly, God really did want Adam and Eve to avoid the Tree of Knowledge. But that brings us back to our question: why would the Lord want to deny humanity an understanding of good and evil?

Catch-22 in the Garden

Actually, the question goes even deeper. It's not simply that it seems strange for God to have put a Tree of Knowledge off-limits to Adam and Eve. Rather, the very existence of such a tree seems to create a basic contradiction in the story as a whole. Here's why:

What happens immediately after Adam and Eve eat from this tree whose fruits confer knowledge of good and evil? The Almighty becomes angry with them and punishes them. But if Adam and Eve were punished for what they did, this presupposes they knew their actions were wrong. You don't punish people who are unaware that they did something bad. So Adam and Eve evidently *had* some knowledge of good and evil before eating from the tree. At the very least, they knew it was right to obey God when He told them not to eat from it, and it was wrong to disobey Him.

But now we're really stuck. For if Adam and Eve already understood the categories of good and evil before reaching for the fruit, well then, they already possessed what the tree was supposed to give them. What, then, would be the purpose of the tree?

It's a catch-22.

This is a very serious dilemma. This is not like wondering why the Torah included an extra word in a verse or why Rashi quoted one Midrash over another. Those are interesting questions, but if you don't have the answer to them, you can still sleep at night. On the other hand, the question we have just raised – *didn't Adam and Eve already have the knowledge the tree was supposed to give them?* – is fundamental. It's basic. It's the kind of question that you *do* lose sleep over. For as long as you are stuck with this question, the story of Adam and Eve simply fails to make any sense at all.

So how are we to deal with this problem? I'd like to sketch the outline of an approach that we may ultimately find useful.

A World Beyond Good and Evil

Perhaps we've been the victims of faulty premises. We've casually assumed that we knew what kind of knowledge the tree gave to Adam and Eve – a knowledge of good and evil, of right and wrong. But on second thought, just because it's called a Tree of Knowledge of Good and Evil doesn't mean that Adam and Eve were ignorant of morality beforehand. It just means that they didn't call morality "knowledge of good and evil." They called it something else.

The approach I am suggesting here is not my own. It is, in fact, the approach taken by Maimonides, the Rambam. Indeed, in his *Guide to the Perplexed*, Rambam considers the very same question we have advanced here: why would God want to withhold

8

knowledge of good and evil from us? And the answer he gives is this: the tree didn't *give* us an understanding of right and wrong when we had none before. Rather it *transformed* this understanding from one thing into another. It transformed our earlier understanding of right and wrong into something called a Knowledge of Good and Evil.

If this seems a little obscure, try thinking about it this way: nowadays, when we do something right, we think of it as "good." And when we do something wrong, we think of it as "evil." But, Rambam contends, those are not the most natural terms one could possibly use. Those terms became relevant to us – they became part of our vocabulary, as it were – only after we ate from the tree and assimilated knowledge of good and evil. In the world of Eden, in the world before "the Tree", the words "good" and "evil" would have seemed strange and inappropriate. Yes, we would have been *aware* of right and wrong, but we would not have called this "good and evil." We would have thought about it differently. We would have called it something else.

What exactly was that "something else"? What would it mean to think about right and wrong in the world of Eden, in the "pre-Tree" world? That, indeed, is the $64,000 question. To some extent, we are reaching beyond ourselves even to ask this question. To ask is to try and understand a world we no longer know, a world in which right and wrong looked, felt, and seemed vastly different than they do now. But try we must, for the Torah suggests that it was *that* world which was the more genuine one. And it is to that world that we strive to return.

Uncovering the nature of right and wrong in the pristine world of Eden will be one of the central tasks before us in the chapters ahead. But before we tackle that complex issue, we need to assemble some more data. So for now, it's back to the drawing board. It's time to explore some of the *other* questions the story of Adam and Eve holds out to us.

ॐ Chapter Two
A Tale of Two Trees

U ntil now, we've concentrated on the mysterious Tree of Knowledge of Good and Evil. But there was more than one special tree in the Garden. For God also created a second, mysterious tree in Paradise – the Tree of Life:

> God made grow out of the ground every tree pleasant to look at and good to eat, [including] the Tree of Life in the middle of the Garden, and the Tree of Knowledge of Good and Evil (Genesis 2:9).

Throughout the Eden story, the Tree of Life remains tantalizingly in the background. It is created but then virtually disappears from the discussion. What role does this second tree play in the story, and how are we to understand its meaning?

Although the Tree of Life may be out of sight, it is not out of mind. Toward the end of the story, after Adam and Eve have eaten the Forbidden Fruit, we once again hear of the Tree of Life:

> God said, 'Man has now become like one of us in knowing good and evil. Now he must be prevented from putting forth

his hand and also taking from the Tree of Life. He [can] eat it and live forever!' (Genesis 3:22).

Here is God's reason for exiling Adam and Eve from Eden. They are sent away to ensure that they will never eat from the Tree of Life. But there's something quite odd about this, for in reading the story we never find that Adam was told to stay away from the Tree of Life in the first place. If God thought it was such an awful idea for humankind to eat from the Tree of Life, why did He not command them to avoid it, as He did concerning the other special tree, the Tree of Knowledge?

Just to complicate matters, the Tree of Life was centrally located in "the middle of the Garden" (Genesis, 2:9), yet Adam and Eve were never warned to avoid its fruit. Indeed, it is unclear whether they even knew that it was a special tree at all. Eventually, what was going to happen? Clearly, it was only a matter of time before someone ate from its fruit.

So the plot thickens. Evidently, God didn't mind Adam and Eve eating from the Tree of Life. He apparently even desired that they eventually eat from it. But all that was *before* eating from the Tree of Knowledge. *After* eating from the Tree of Knowledge, somehow, everything changes. Now, the Tree of Life becomes off-limits. Every effort must be taken to ensure that humankind never eats from it.

Why? What accounts for this curious relationship between the trees? Why is the Tree of Life fine to eat from *before* partaking from the Tree of Knowledge, but not after? That's one point we'll want to return to. But we're not done yet exploring the mysterious relationship between these two trees. Indeed, we are just beginning.

The Cherubs with the Flaming Sword

When God expels the humans from the Garden, the Almighty places angels with a flaming sword at the entrance to "guard the way [back to] the Tree of Life" (Genesis 3:24). These angels are of a very particular kind. They are cherubs. (For those of you who enjoy Renaissance art, that's the kind of angel that Rubens always liked to paint, although I don't know why he thought he knew what they looked like.) Now, as it happens, a cherub is a relatively rare kind of angel. Throughout the entire Five Books of Moses, we find them only in two places. Besides their appearance here, guarding the Tree of Life, they are mentioned just once more. Placed atop the Holy Ark in the Tabernacle are two cherubs, fashioned out of gold: "Make two golden cherubs, hammering them out from the two ends [of the ark]... The cherubs shall spread their wings upward so that their wings shield the [ark's] cover..." (*Exodus* 25:18; 25:20).

Now go one step farther. What treasure was this second pair of cherubs guarding – these only other cherubs in the entire Five Books of Moses? They were, of course, guarding the Ten Commandments that were inside the ark. They were guarding the Torah. Those who attend synagogue on the Sabbath will be familiar with the words I am thinking of right now. You say them every week, as the Torah is raised aloft from the *bima* for all to see: "It is a tree of life to all who grab hold of it" (*Proverbs* 3:18).

Fascinating. The only other time we meet cherubs in the entire Chumash, they are once again guarding a "Tree of Life." Only this time, they are not keeping us *away* from the Tree of Life; they are ushering us towards it, shielding both us and the Torah beneath their protective wings.

What are we to make of this? Why are the cherubs who keep us away from the original Tree of Life trying to give us access to a second such tree? What does it even mean to call the Torah "a Tree of Life"? Is there an essential similarity between the two?

The skeptic inside you might dismiss all this as coincidence. Cherubs here, cherubs there, cherubs, cherubs, everywhere. But if we explore further, we will find that there are still other links that connect the Torah with the Tree of Life...

Do the Tree of Knowledge and the Tree of Life Contradict Each Other?

Try this question on for size: What were Adam and Eve like before eating from either tree, the Tree of Knowledge or the Tree of Life? Were they mortal or immortal?

We know that Adam was warned not to eat from the Tree of Knowledge, because "on the day that you eat from it, you will surely die" (Genesis 2:17). The classic commentator Nachmanides observes that the verse can't mean that the fruit immediately kills you, for, in fact, Adam and Eve went on to live for a long time after eating the Forbidden Fruit. Rather, the verse seems to mean "on the day that you eat from the fruit *you will become mortal*," i.e. you will immediately become transformed into beings that eventually die. This, apparently, is the meaning of God's warning.

So the Tree of Knowledge proves that Adam and Eve were originally immortal, right? Wrong. Let's see what the Tree of Life adds to our understanding.

The Torah tells us that God banished Adam and Eve from Eden "lest they eat from the Tree of Life and live forever." Well, the verse seems pretty clear: the fruit of the Tree of Life confers immortality. Once you eat it, you will never die. So if the Tree of Life *makes* you immortal – well, that seems to mean you were mortal beforehand.

But wait a minute. I thought we said just a minute ago that Adam and Eve started out being *immortal*.

Something strange is going on with these trees. The Tree of Knowledge seems to tell us that man would originally have lived forever. But the Tree of Life seems to tell us that he was originally a being that would die. At face value, the two trees seem to contradict themselves.

But only at face value. There's a way out of the contradiction. A surprising alternative exists about the original nature of Adam and Eve that would resolve the problem.

The Garden of Eden and
the Heisenberg Uncertainty Principle

The alternative is this: both trees are right. Mankind, before eating from either tree, was neither mortal nor immortal. If he ate from the Tree of Life, he would *become* immortal; if he ate from the Tree of Knowledge, he would *become* a being that dies. In that moment, though, before eating from either tree, he was in the "twilight zone." He was perched precariously between mortality and immortality, but, as of yet, his nature was undetermined.

If such an "undetermined state" seems strange to you, don't fret. Just repair to the library and pick up any book on quantum physics. According to this branch of science, it is a pretty standard feature of reality for things to be undetermined. At any one moment, a given electron may be here, or it may be there, Heisenberg famously proclaimed, but right now it is neither here nor there. Its position becomes "determined" only once an observer steps in and looks at it. Well, if electrons can remain undetermined, maybe people can as well.

Now, if we're right about all of this – that Eden was a place where Adam was precariously placed between life and death, depending on his choice – well, then, it would seem that Eden eerily foreshadows another great moment of Jewish history. It reminds us of another, later time, when we were neither here nor there, and the Almighty offered us a similar choice between life and death: "See! Today I have set before you [a free choice] between life and good [on one side], and death and evil [on the other]....Now therefore, choose life!" (Deuteronomy 30:14,19).

When Moses uttered these words, the people stood in the wasteland of a desert, not yet possessing either the "life" or the "death" that lay before them. On that occasion, too, we were asked to choose. In that case, "life" was identified as embracing the Torah and its principles, while "death" meant rejecting them.

Strange. The choice to embrace the Torah or reject it is painted with the same brush as the choice to embrace the Tree of Life. The cherubs that guard one tree guard the other "tree," the Torah. It might be just a coincidence, a convenient choice of metaphors. But it might also signify something deeper. What could it all mean?

We have a long way to go, but we are starting to get somewhere in developing our picture of the two mysterious trees in Eden. In upcoming chapters, we will lay out some other puzzle pieces in the grand saga of Adam and Eve in Eden. And then, once the jigsaw pieces are all out on the floor, we'll begin, bit by bit, to discern the picture they reveal.

೬ Chapter Three
The Dark Side of Paradise

The Bible is rife with conflict between characters who exemplify good and evil. While our sympathies may lie with whichever characters align themselves with the "good," these characters are not always the center of the story. Consider, as an example, the narrative of Cain and Abel. The story isn't about Abel. We know virtually nothing about him – he is killed, and he disappears. Like it or not, the story is really about Cain. What brought him to murder another person? What did his inner world look like? What did God mean to tell him just before he killed his brother? And did he really ever achieve forgiveness?

Who are the main characters in the story of the Forbidden Fruit in the Garden of Eden? Our first impulse is to point to Adam and Eve. But maybe the story is about someone else, too – the snake. He's not a very popular being, certainly not a hero, but perhaps the story is about him almost as much as it is about us. Let's spend some time trying to understand his role in the story.

What Do We Know About the Snake?
In teaching this story before various audiences, I find that students often speculate about the identity of the snake. Some peg

him as "the Devil" – a sort of fallen angel, a powerful "enemy of God" who seeks to thwart the divine plan at every turn. As a Jew, I have difficulty with the notion of an independent source of evil in the universe serving as a counterweight to God. Jewish thought tends to see Satan in different terms, not as one who opposes the divine plan, but as a sort of "heavenly prosecutor," who is part and parcel of the divine plan. Just as no earthly court is complete without a prosecutor, so too, the Heavenly Court is incomplete without its "prosecutor," a being who forcefully advocates for the application of divine justice in full rigor.

Was the snake, then, a manifestation of an angelic Satan – whoever this Satan is? Maybe, but when I read the text, I see an animal here. One could argue that the angel is disguised in the form of an animal, but let's at least give it a whirl and see if we can make the text understandable without resort to Satan. Let's say the snake is an animal. What does he want? How are we to understand him?

Let's begin by gathering some pertinent information. From the text of the Torah, what do we know about this snake? Well, for starters, he talks – not very snake-like at all. And to make matters worse, we're not even supposed to be *surprised* that he talks. When, for example, the Torah relates the story of Bila'am and his talking donkey (Numbers 23), we are clearly meant to be surprised by the animal's speech. But here in Genesis, the snake's capacity for language just seems to be a given. The Torah tells us that one day a snake approached Eve and happened to strike up a conversation. Don't be surprised. That's just the way it is.

And it gets even more puzzling. The snake doesn't only talk. He walks, too. We know this because at the end of the story, the snake is cursed by God – and the curse states that from this point forward, the snake must crawl on his belly and eat dust. The implication is clear: before that point, the snake was *not* a creature that crawled. He walked.

Let's go still further. What did this walking, talking creature eat before he was cursed? We don't know, but evidently it wasn't "dust" – *that* only became his diet afterward. As the snake was originally created, he seems meant to dine on something more appealing.

And what about the intelligence level of this creature? The Torah is clear about that. The snake, according to the text, was pretty bright: "And the snake was more cunning than any beast of the field" (Genesis 3:1).

So let's add it all up. The snake walks. The snake talks. He likes good food. He is intelligent. What does he remind you of?

I don't know about you, but he reminds me of a human being.

Indeed, the snake so closely resembles a human that he forces us to ask: *what, in the end, makes him a snake and not a human?* This question hits close to home, because it's really a question about us and the nature of our humanity. Bottom line: what makes *us* human and not a snake? If you walk, talk and are smart, are you then a person? Or can you still be a snake?

The snake forces us to ask: where is the essential dividing line between human and animal?

A Curious Temptation

But the mystery of the serpent does not end there. What else is strange about how the Torah portrays him in the story?

Well, there is what this talking snake actually *says*. Remember, the Torah describes the snake as a smart operator, very "cunning." So pretend, for a moment, that you were the snake, and you were very smart, and you wanted to coax Eve into eating some fruit she shouldn't be eating. How would you go about it?

Maybe you'd tell Eve how delicious the fruit looks. Maybe you'd craft a seductive lie about its mysterious powers. Maybe, like the Evil Queen in Snow White, you'd just show up at her doorstep with a shiny apple.

But let's see what the snake actually does. He approaches Eve, and, in the original Hebrew, says the following words: "*af ki amar elokim lo tochlu mikol etz hagan.*" Most translations render these words: "Did God really say that you may not eat from any of the trees of the Garden?" (Genesis 3:1).

But that's not a precise translation of the Hebrew. A better, more literal translation would read: "Even if God said do not eat from any of the trees of the Garden…"

Well, it's no wonder that most translations take liberties with the Hebrew; the basic, literal translation of these words is quite strange, to say the least. First of all, the sentence has no ending. It just trails off into nothingness, as if the snake were interrupted before he could get to the punch-line. But even if we help the snake finish his thought, his words are hardly more understandable. For what he seems to be telling Eve is: "Even if God said don't eat from any trees of the Garden, so what? Do it anyway!"

One second. The best possible argument the snake could come up with was: "Even if God said don't do it, so what?" That doesn't seem very cunning, does it? Of all things, why choose to *remind* Eve that she's not supposed to eat the fruit? Why flippantly suggest that she disregard her Creator's command? Remember: to Eve, God is not just some abstract concept. God is real; God quite literally created her. What kind of argument is: "Even if God said no, so what?"

To Be As God

Continue reading, and the snake's argument takes another interesting twist. Let's listen in as the snake suggests to Eve that he knows the *real* reason God forbade her and Adam to eat the fruit: "Really, God knows that on the day that you eat from it, your eyes will be opened and you will be like God, knowing good and evil" (Genesis 3:5).

Ponder this for a moment, and then ask yourself: is the snake lying or telling the truth? I don't know about you, but at first blush, it sure seemed to me that he was lying. I could hear my mind work: What kind of preposterous nonsense is it to suggest that God is jealously guarding the Tree of Knowledge because it holds the key to being godly? Is God really so territorial, worried that lowly humans, by virtue of eating some fruit, would magically become just like Him and encroach upon His heavenly realm? Please. The snake *must* be lying.

But there's no reason to philosophize about it. The text itself reveals to us whether the snake was lying or telling the truth. The verse I'm thinking of appears after Adam and Eve have eaten the Forbidden Fruit. Reflecting on their failure, God declares to Himself that mankind must now be banished entirely from the Garden. And here's the reason why: "God said, 'Man has now become like one of us in knowing good and evil. Now he must be prevented from putting forth his hand and also taking from the Tree of Life. He [can] eat it and live forever!'" (3:22).

As impossible as it seems, the snake *was* telling the truth after all. It's black on white. God clearly states that the fruit has somehow elevated Adam and Eve to become "like" Him, as they are now "knowers of good and evil." But how could it be? If the Tree of Knowledge really does make one godly, wouldn't the Almighty want us to have it? It seems pretty blasphemous to suggest that God was afraid of competition from the creatures He Himself created. *not really. there was Lucifer*

Finally, as if this statement of God were not already perplexing enough, there's one last thing that's odd about it. Listen to how, in this verse, God defines what it means to be a divine being: "Man has now become like one of us, knowing good and evil" (Genesis 3:22).

Ask ten people on the street for a one-sentence definition of God. You'll probably hear that God is All-powerful. That God is All-knowing. That God is One. Or that God is the Creator. Would anyone tell you that being God means "knowing good and evil"? But that's precisely what the Almighty Himself says.

The snake – this walking, talking representative of the animal world – is right. God Himself confirms the snake's words. Being godly means knowing good and evil. Now it is up to us to find out what both God and the snake meant.

𝒞 Chapter Four
The Naked Truth

The entire story of Adam and Eve in the Garden is no more than twenty-five verses long. That's a pretty small amount of space in which to tell a story that changed the course of human history. The *Encyclopedia Britannica* would have devoted dozens of pages to an event of such magnitude. How can the Torah communicate anything really profound in so few words?

One way the Torah communicates so concisely is by creating more than one layer of meaning in its narrative. Twenty-five verses may not sound like a lot, but it's plenty if the text is somehow layered, encoded so that it contains meaning far out of proportion to its size. Jewish tradition has long understood that the Torah employs various techniques to help it encode meaning. One of those techniques is a device that's come to be known as the *leading word* [*milah hamanchah*].

Every once in a while, when you are reading a biblical narrative, you will find that the text seems to go out of its way to use a certain word, phrase or idea, consistently and repetitively throughout a story. When this happens, it often indicates that this repetitive element holds a key to the meaning of the narrative. The word or idea in question *leads* the reader, as it were, to a richer and deeper understanding of the text.

It just so happens that the story of Adam and Eve in the Garden contains such a repetitive word. If you take a quick break to scan the story yourself, you may well find it.

It is the Hebrew word *arom*, "nakedness."

The Strange Prominence of Nakedness

Nakedness appears everywhere throughout our story. It appears at the beginning, just before the snake tempts Adam and Eve: "And they were both naked, the man and his wife, and they were not ashamed" (Genesis, 2:24). It appears at the end, when God makes clothes for Adam and Eve so that they are no longer naked (Genesis, 3:21). And it appears right in the middle of the story, at its turning point, when husband and wife eat the Forbidden Fruit: "And the eyes of both of them were open and they knew that they were naked" (Genesis, 3:11).

Strange, isn't it? If someone asked you to imagine how eating a fruit that imparts "knowledge of good and evil" would affect mankind, what would you have said? Perhaps Adam and Eve would become instantly aware of a whole new world of moral dilemmas lying before them: the Right to Life vs. Right to Choice; or: ten people are in a lifeboat and the whole boat sinks unless you throw someone off; what should you do? There are all sorts of such dilemmas. Their heads would be spinning with possibilities.

But no, none of that preoccupied Adam and Eve. When they ate from the Tree of Knowledge, the immediate effect was: *they knew that they were naked*. It seems odd. Why does knowing "good and evil" affect our perception of nakedness? Whatever the explanation, there is no denying that nakedness is central to the story.

Let's continue reading the text. Adam eats from the tree and immediately hides from God. Why is he hiding?

Before looking at the reason given in the text – under the circumstances, why do *you* think Adam would hide? Imagine that some industrious CNN reporter has managed to spot Adam hiding behind a bush and gotten an exclusive interview with him. He asks Adam a basic question: "I see you are crouching here behind this bush; you seem to be hiding from God. Can you explain to our viewers why?" If you were in Adam's shoes, what you say in reply?

You probably would tell the reporter that you are embarrassed because of what you have done. Here you are, placed in Paradise, with the whole Garden available to you for your enjoyment. One little thing God has asked of you – not to eat from a certain tree. And then you had to go and eat from it! You feel filled with shame; you've disappointed your Creator and can't bear to face Him. If you are hiding, one would think that this would be the reason why.

But the text tells us something else. When God asked Adam why he was hiding, this was his reply: "I heard your voice in the Garden, and I hid because I was *naked*."

Somehow, Adam's consciousness of being naked was so profound, so disturbing to him, that it trumped even his sense of shame at having disobeyed the one command of his Maker. Why is nakedness so important to this story? Why is humanity's realization of it the one natural consequence of eating from a Tree of Knowledge? And why would this realization be so disturbing that it is the only reason Adam can think of to explain why he is hiding?

In order to answer these questions, we need to realize that we haven't yet seen the end of nakedness in this story. It actually makes one more hidden appearance. Believe it or not, there's one more creature in the Garden that's naked, and he may hold the key we have been seeking. Can you spot him?

A Phantom Nakedness

If you had trouble identifying the phantom nakedness in our story, it was probably because you were reading the story in English. As it happens, most English translations, almost without exception, conceal the missing occurrence of nakedness. They usually render the telltale verses something like this: "And they were both naked, the man and his wife, and they were not ashamed. Now the serpent was more cunning than any beast of the field…" (Genesis 2:25–3:1).

As you read these words, you surely noticed that Adam and Eve were described as unclothed. But you probably didn't observe anyone else described the same way. Now trust me on this one. You didn't see it because you were reading the words in English. Try reading the verses now, when we substitute the Hebrew word for "naked" – *arom* – in place of its English counterpart:

> And they were both arom, the man and his wife, and they
>   were not ashamed.
> Now the serpent was more arom than any beast of the
>   field…
>
> (Genesis, 2:25–3:1).

One second. The snake is arom, too? Absolutely. Immediately after the Torah describes Adam and Eve as naked, the Torah uses the exact same Hebrew term to describe the snake. It just so happens that arom can mean not just *naked*, but *cunning*, too.

Well, what are we to make of this? In its simple meaning, the text is telling us about the crafty intentions of the snake – that he is cunning, sly and deceitful. But it hardly seems a coincidence the Torah picked *this particular word* – arom – to describe the snake's devious intentions. The Torah goes out of its way to attach this very key word in the story to the cunning snake.

The mystery deepens when we ask: Are the two meanings of arom – "naked" and "cunning" – related conceptually in any way? Are these apples and elephants, two entirely unrelated ideas, or do they have some essential connection?

At first glance, the ideas "naked" and "cunning" don't seem to have much in common. But on reflection, they *do* seem related in a curious way. Mull the terms over – "naked and cunning, naked and cunning…" – what comes to mind?

These words just happen to be opposites of one another.

When someone is naked, unclothed, there is no hiding. That person's self is laid bare for all to see. "What you see is what you get." On the other hand, when one is cunning, he is sly and devious; he "cloaks" his true intentions and hides behind a facade. His true self is not seen.

Fascinating; the two meanings of arom are mirror images of each other.

All this adds another dimension to our question: why would the Torah take a word it uses over and over again to mean "naked" and then, when describing the snake, twist that word's meaning to convey the very opposite idea – "cunning"?

Could the Torah be suggesting that – yes, the snake was, of course, cunning; but, somehow, he was not *just* cunning – he was naked as well? What could this mean?

An Innocent Deception

Biologically, of course, a snake really *is* naked. It is a reptile, a creature that, unlike most other members of the animal kingdom, lacks fur or hair to cover it. But if we think beyond biology, what would it mean for the snake to be not just cunning, but naked?

If "naked" really is the opposite of "cunning", then it follows that the snake had both opposing qualities: he possessed both honesty and stealth. In other words, the snake really *is* deceptive; but, on another, perhaps deeper, level, he's very straightforward. It all depends how you look at him. From one perspective, what he's saying doesn't really apply to Adam and Eve, so his words are deceptive to them. But from another perspective, "what you see is what you get." He's just telling it like it is – from a snake's point of view, of course.

It happens that this perspective fits like a glove with a number of other clues scattered throughout our story. But we're getting ahead of ourselves, for we are not quite done yet exploring the snake's crafty disposition. There's one more important question we haven't asked yet: What's in it for the snake?

ॐ Chapter Five

What's In It for the Snake?

The Torah describes the snake as being sly or devious. But whenever we talk about someone acting slyly or deviously, we always mean that they are sly and devious *in pursuit of some goal*. With the snake, that piece of the puzzle is missing. We know that he is sly, but that is all the text says about him. We have no clue what his motive for the crime might be. To put it succinctly: "What's in it for the snake?"

Perhaps the Torah doesn't reveal the snake's motivation because it is obvious. In other words, perhaps the snake's motivation is there for all to see – if we just take the time to view his temptation in context. That is, the serpent doesn't come out of nowhere with his offer of fruit to Eve. There is a history to his offer. Discerning that history is a key to understanding not just the snake, but the story of the Forbidden Fruit as a whole.

Where Does Our Story Begin?

Most of us think that the story of the Forbidden Fruit begins in chapter three, when the serpent shows up, engages Eve in conversation, and tempts her to eat what she shouldn't be eating. But, in truth, that's not the beginning of the story. The story actually begins a bit earlier, when the Tree of Knowledge is first introduced and the command to avoid it is first given:

> Out of the ground God caused to grow every tree pleasant to the sight and good for food; the Tree of Life in the middle of the Garden, and the Tree of Knowledge of Good and Evil (2:9). And the Lord God commanded Adam, saying 'Of every tree of the Garden you may eat freely. But of the Tree of Knowledge of Good and Evil you shall not eat...' (2:16–17).

It's easy to miss the fact that the story actually begins in the prior chapter, because following the introduction of the two trees, the text inexplicably digresses. After we first hear of the two trees, God declares that "it is not good for man to be alone," and the Almighty then sets about trying to find a helpmate for him. The Almighty creates all the beasts of the field and parades them before Adam, who names all the creatures but has no success finding a mate among them. Finally, the Lord puts Adam to sleep and takes a rib from him, out of which God builds Eve. And only then, *after* the text tells us about the creation of both Eve and the animals, does the story return to the Forbidden Fruit. Our familiar snake comes along, offers the fruit to Eve, and the rest is history.

All in all, it's a strange path for the text to take. Why does Adam's search for a mate interrupt the story about the Tree of Knowledge? It would seem more logical to get the creation of Eve and the animals out of the way first, and *then* begin talking about the Tree of Knowledge; that way, the narrator could bring each story to its conclusion without interruption. But for some reason, the Torah doesn't do it this way. It places the creation of the animals and Eve right in the middle of the Tree of Knowledge narrative. Why?

Let's begin by examining this "digression" a little more closely. The truth is, the story it tells is quite bizarre in its own right. Put yourself, for a moment, in the "shoes" of the Almighty. Imagine that you had created Adam and were then concerned that he not be all alone. You decide he needs a helpmate. What's the next thing you would do?

You'd probably decide to create Eve.

But that's not what happens. Instead, the Almighty creates all the beasts of the field and brings them before Adam to see if he will find an appropriate mate among them. One by one, Adam rejects them. During that effort, Adam names each of the animals. Now, let's stop a minute to ask: Why, exactly, did God perform this little experiment? Are we to believe that God, the Great Match-maker in the Sky, couldn't figure out that a zebra wouldn't be a good match for Adam? And after the zebra didn't work out as a wife, was it really necessary to try the hippopotamus and the fla-mingo also? Why is this odd episode told, and why does it inter-rupt the story of the tree?

Maybe the Digression Is Really Part of the Story

The combined weight of these questions suggests that we may have been too hasty in classifying God's attempt to find a mate for Adam as a digression. Perhaps this thread is *not* an interruption of the Tree of Knowledge narrative at all. Instead, I'd like to suggest that the creation of the beasts of the field – and Adam's rejection of them – is actually crucial to the entire Forbidden Fruit narra-tive. In particular, I am going to argue that it is utterly impossible to understand the snake and his temptation without all this.

We were puzzled earlier about the snake's motive. He is cun-ning, but to what end? Well, perhaps the Torah doesn't talk about the snake's motivation because it's clear from the context. The dis-cussion of possible companions for Adam, I would suggest, pro-vides the missing motive for the snake. In other words, perhaps it was Adam's rejection of the animals in favor of Eve that propelled the snake into action.

Remember how God had brought all the beasts of the field – *chayat hasadeh*, as the verse calls them – before Adam to see if he could find a mate among them? It turns out that chayat hasadeh is a relatively rare phrase. It appears in only one other context in the

31

entire Book of Genesis – in the description of the snake. When we first meet this primal serpent, the Torah describes the creature as "more cunning than *all the beasts of the field* [chayat hasadeh]."

This phrase may be the clue to what drives this walking, talking serpent. As the representative of the animal world that is closest, as it were, to Adam, the snake was attempting to succeed where all other animals had failed. All the other chayat hasadeh had been unsuccessful in providing companionship for Adam. The snake, however, was more cunning than those chayat hasadeh: he was seeking to convince the human that at least one beast of the field would be a fitting companion, after all.

A fascinating and perplexing ancient midrashic text seems to suggest precisely this. The Sages of the Midrash were puzzled, as we were, with the missing motivation of the serpent. What drives him? Their answer is shocking. They say that the snake was on an assassination mission. Knowing that the Forbidden Fruit harbored the promise of death, the snake hoped that Eve would pass the fruit to Adam before partaking herself. Why? Because according to the Midrash, the snake wanted to assassinate Adam and marry Eve (Bereishit Rabbah, 18:6, as cited by Rashi to 3:1).

At face value, the Midrash seems preposterous. "Assassinate Adam and marry Eve? What would the children look like?" you protest. But let me offer a quick word to the wise: the Midrash frequently speaks in the language of allegory, and it intentionally cloaks its message in metaphoric garb. Traditional commentators from Luzzatto to Maharal have rarely taken the statements of the Midrash literally. The sages often convey deep truths through the mysterious, allegorical garb of Midrash.

Perhaps this particular midrashic teaching is trying to lead us toward the very conclusion we have gingerly been approaching ourselves – namely, that the snake's offer results from Adam's choice to reject the animals in favor of Eve. In consequence of that rejection, the animal world – with the snake as its representative – leveled a challenge to the first humans: "What makes you so special? What makes *you* so *different from us* that you stand alone and require one another as mates? We can be your soul-mates, too…"

It Is Not Good for Man to Be Alone

Let's explore this notion a bit further. The Almighty had given Adam dominion over the animal world. As such, Adam had been set apart from that world in a very fundamental way. The human was atop Creation but was all alone in this powerful and dominating position: "And then God said: It is not good for man to be alone. I will make him a helpmate to join with him."

Isolated, in charge of a vast world of nature, Adam sees himself as different, in some fundamental way, from every other creature around him. He is a ruler, yes – but a ruler who is not fully kindred with his subjects. He is alone. The temptation of loneliness is to seek solace where it ought not to be sought. For Adam, this would mean seeking companionship among the animals, pretending, if only he could, that he is one of them.

The animal world, for its part, might be seen as only too happy to oblige. If animals could think rational thoughts, if we could anthropomorphize the perspective of the animal world, what opinions might they have about our dominion over them? If animals could challenge our right to dominate, how would they do so?

The implicit challenge of the animal world is: "Are you really so different from us, that you stand above us? At your core, aren't you really one of us?" And it's not just a question that animals might ask. It's a question we could all ask ourselves, every time we exert control over an animal – every time we harness an ox to a plow or saddle up a horse to ride upon: "Who am I to do this? Am I really so different?"

The snake gives a voice to these doubts. "Are you really so sure you need a human as a companion?" it whispers. "Why not choose a soul-mate from *our* world?" Earlier I asked facetiously what the children of such a union might look like. But that's precisely the point. They would be "snake-people." The snake would

33

have co-opted the world of humans and made it part and parcel of the animal kingdom.

The Almighty, however, gave Adam a chance to experience how futile it would be to find real companionship in the animal world. It wasn't God but Adam who needed to be shown this. In allowing Adam to name and search for a mate among the animals, God was seeking to inoculate humanity from the temptation it would soon face, to convince Adam through experience that he could never really be one with the animal world. Only after such a trial could Adam truly appreciate the unique compatibility of Eve – "a bone from my bones; flesh from my flesh" (2:23). And only after Adam's trial is humanity ready for the challenge of the serpent: "Aren't you one of us?"

All of this brings us back to a question we entertained earlier, a question we've not yet answered squarely: "What, really, is the dividing line between human and animal?" The very existence of the snake raises this issue. The primal serpent walks. He talks. And he's clever. So in what sense is he really a snake and not a human? Why *couldn't* he be a fitting mate for Eve, after all?

The real answer to this question, I think, lies buried in the heart of our story. Let's try to unearth it.

ℓ Chapter Six

Beauty and the Beast

The snake's challenge to Eve is critical for discovering the essential difference between snake and human. We asked earlier about the strangeness of the snake's opening words to Eve: "Even if God said not to eat from any trees of the Garden…" From there, the sentence trails off into nothingness, as if the snake were interrupted before he could finish the thought. But let's try to reconstruct the end of the sentence. The snake seems to be saying: "Even if God said don't eat, *so what? Do it anyway!*" Okay, stop the tape – let's look at this: where, exactly, is the temptation here?

I'd like to share with you an approach proposed by Rabbi Samson Raphael Hirsch, a giant of biblical exegesis, who lived a little over a century ago. Hirsch suggested that understanding the snake's words is a matter of emphasis; or, to put it another way, it is a matter of where one puts italics in the sentence. Above, we read the verse as: "Even if God said don't eat, *so what?*" Hirsch asked, "What if we read it differently, with the emphasis placed on the word *said?*"

The sentence sounds a whole lot different now: "Even if God *said* don't eat, so what?" Read this way, the snake isn't really challenging the authority of God, per se. His argument is much more

35

limited; he's just saying that God's spoken words are not the things you should pay attention to. To paraphrase Hirsch, the snake would be saying something like the following:

> God may have *said* to avoid the tree, but the question is: 'Do you want to eat from the tree? Do you desire it?' And let's say you *do* desire the tree. Where do you think those desires came from? Who put them inside you? Wasn't God the one who put them inside you? Certainly He did....He is your Maker.

All in all, the snake is pointing to a great and terrible contra- diction. On the one hand, God's voice instructs you not to eat of the tree. But on the other hand, another voice of God – His voice inside you; your passions, your desires – beckons you indeed to eat of the tree.

So, to which voice should you listen – the voice of God that comes to you in words, or the voice of God that pulses inside you, that animates your very being? Which divine voice is more primary?

"I don't know about you," the snake says, "but, if I were in your shoes, here's how I would see it. Even if God *said* don't eat of the trees, so what? It's not the voice that speaks to you *in words* that's primary. It's the voice *inside you* that's primary!"

The Naked Snake

In saying this, the snake is not necessarily being malicious or even devious. On the contrary, he can be seen as very innocent, very straightforward – very naked. After all, he's just telling you what it's like to be a snake.

Consider this: How does God make His Will known to a snake? How, for that matter, does God make His Will known to any animal? The Almighty doesn't instruct animals intellectu- ally, doesn't speak to them in words. There is no Bible, no Torah, revealed atop a mountain for snakes, birds, and lizards. But just because a snake doesn't have a law book doesn't mean no laws exist for him. To the contrary, animals follow the Divine Will quite faithfully. The voice of God beats palpably inside of them. God speaks to animals through the passions, desires, and instincts they find within themselves. Every time a grizzly bear goes salmon hunting in an Alaskan river; every time worker bees chase the drones out of a hive – every time an animal acts "naturally," obeying the voice of instinct or desire within itself – the animal follows the Will of its Creator.

So for the snake, the way out of the apparent contradiction is quite clear: "Even if God *said* don't eat from the tree, so what?" The real voice of God is not to be found in words. The real voice of God doesn't speak to you from the outside, it pulses insistently within you.

And that is the essential temptation of the serpent. It is a temptation that cuts to the core of our humanity. Remember how we asked before: Why is it that the snake could never be a fitting companion for Adam? How is humanity fundamentally different from the snake, or, for that matter, from any member of the animal world? Well, let's try and tackle that now.

Does our uniqueness as humans lie in the fact that we can talk? Perhaps. But if we met a talking animal, would we grant it human rights? Lately, researchers have taught limited sign language to apes. Would these apes qualify as furry humans?

Maybe our advanced intelligence is what makes us human. But what if we met a really smart animal? As I understand it, the jury is still out on the intelligence of dolphins. If dolphins really are as bright as some claim, should they be entitled to the right to vote?

Well, then, if the key to our humanity doesn't lie in our capacity for speech, for walking on two legs, or for intelligent thinking – all of which were shared by our friend, the primal serpent – in what *does* our humanity lie? I would argue that it lies in how you answer this one query: "How does God speak to you? Which is the primary voice of God?"

If God speaks to you primarily through passion and instinct; if all you need to do is examine your desires to find out what God wants of you; if your essential self is easily and naturally identified with your passions – well, you are an animal. If you are able to stand outside your passions and examine them critically; if desire is something you *have*, not something you *are*; if God addresses Himself to your mind and asks you to rise above your desires, or to channel them constructively – well, then you are a human.

What the snake is really doing, then, is forcing Adam and Eve to confront what it means for them to be human beings and not beasts. In the end, the snake really is "arom" – in both senses of the word. When he asks, "Even if God *said* don't eat, so what?" he is being straightforward and honest – *naked*, as it were. He is just telling it like it is: "Here's what it is like to be a snake." On the other hand, when we look at the snake's words from *our* point of view, namely from the perspective of Adam and Eve, then his argument looks cunning and deceptive, the other meaning of "arom." What's right for the snake is not necessarily right for us. He may walk; he may talk; he may be smart – but we are different from him; we hear a voice that is not relevant to him. When all is said and done, we are more than the sum total of our instincts or passions. We are not snakes.

Beauty and the Beast

Before making her decision to take the fruit, Eve contemplated the choice before her. According to the text, here is what happened: "And the woman saw that the tree was good to eat, and that it was a delight to the eyes, and that the tree was desirable as a means to wisdom" (Genesis, 3:6).

That, at least, is how most translations render the verses; and, indeed, it is how some commentators interpret them. But the Hebrew indicates otherwise. A more literal translation of the last phrase, *venechmad ha'etz lehaskil*, yields not that the tree was *"desirable as a means to wisdom"* but that it was *"desirable to contemplate"* (Genesis 3:6).

"Desirable to contemplate" – it's a strange phrase, and maybe that's why many translations shun it. What does it mean; what kinds of things are desirable to contemplate? For that matter, how does this last phrase fit with the first two? Are the three phrases – "good to eat"/ "delight to the eyes"/ "desirable to contemplate" – all related somehow?

I think they are. All three describe how the tree appealed to Eve *aesthetically* – at the level of beauty; or, more precisely, at the level of desire. Each description portrays in what way the fruit was "desirable." Each description is more sophisticated, more subtle than the last.

To explain: A lollipop tastes "good to eat." Even a two-year-old child can appreciate that. But it takes a ten-year-old to appreciate the beauty of a rose – beauty that is "a delight to the eyes," not to the mouth. And what about things that are "desirable to contemplate"? This is beauty that appeals not to any of our physical senses, but to our mind. The poems of Emily Dickinson, the symphonies of Beethoven, an elegant debating performance – all these are "desirable to contemplate." They appeal to the mind, yes, but not because they are *true* – rather, because they are *beautiful*. Indeed, a poem may or may not express a truth, and a good debater can be impressive even if he's lying through his teeth. But that's irrelevant. The mind appreciates the beauty of such things – and desires them accordingly.

The tree appealed to Eve at all aesthetic levels from the most obvious to the most subtle and refined. The fruit of the tree was dripping with allure. "Even if God *said* don't eat, so what?"

You Are What You Eat

The snake's challenge to eat the Forbidden Fruit followed naturally from his belief that the voice of desire is the primary way God speaks to us, that desire and instinct are more trustworthy indicators of God's Will than God's words. From his perspective, the snake's argument is very natural, very innocent: "Eat from the tree, Eve, internalize your desires, find your center in them, and you shall truly be godly."

*   *   *

But what, you ask, does all this have to do with "knowing good and evil"? Why would a battle over the proper role of desire in the human psyche be waged over a tree that contains, of all things, "knowledge of good and evil"?

Hang on. We'll explore that next.

ℯ Chapter Seven
A World of Broccoli and Pizza

The time has come to examine more carefully the centerpiece of our story, the "Tree of Knowledge." Doing so, however, is no easy task. The tree isn't around anymore, and even if it were, we probably couldn't understand it by taking sap samples from its trunk or by measuring the biochemical qualities of its fruit. But while the tree itself is gone, the Hebrew words that describe its characteristics are alive and well. And these, I think, hold some important clues. The forbidden tree is known in Hebrew as *Etz HaDa'at Tov Vara*. The conventional translation of the phrase is "knowledge of good and evil." Let's explore what the name really means.

What Is Real Knowledge Made Of?
We'll start with the first phrase *da'at*, routinely translated as "knowledge." The meaning of this word, however, is not limited to conventional knowledge. Indeed, one of the first times in Genesis this Hebrew root appears, it conveys an experience that, at first blush, few of us would call "knowledge" at all:

*V'ha'adam **yada** et chavah ishto...*
And the man **knew** his wife... (Genesis 4:1).

In the Bible, the word da'at doubles as a synonym for sexual intimacy. The Torah's use of this word for both "knowledge" and "sexual union" is no doubt significant. More than likely, there is a core understanding of "da'at" that gives rise to both these meanings. What would that core be about?

Let's approach it this way: When a man "knows" his wife, what is he really seeking? Cynics might reply that he's after nothing but pleasure. But beyond sheer physical pleasure – even beyond procreation – is there not something more, something deeper, that he seeks? Perhaps, on some level, he is indeed after "knowledge" – knowledge of the mysterious, alluring feminine that is so different from him, but so much a "missing part" of him at the same time. To be sure, it is not intellectual knowledge that he seeks. He is seeking raw, first-hand knowledge. He is seeking to *experience* the feminine in a direct, unfiltered way.

In the branch of philosophy known as epistemology, a long-standing debate has raged about what real "knowledge" consists of. Rationalists have argued that "head knowledge" reigns supreme. You know something is true when you can demonstrate it through logic or analysis. Other philosophers, however, have asserted that real knowledge is only gained by experience. It's all very nice to contemplate an idea in your head, they contend, but you only know it's real when it happens in the real world; when you demonstrate it, say, in a laboratory. If you see it, if you feel it, if you *experience* it – then you know it's real.

Da'at seems to denote this latter kind of knowledge – knowing something by experiencing it. A scientist who performs an experiment attains da'at, even though he can't yet explain the rationale behind what he has experienced. A man attains da'at of a woman by joining with her and experiencing her, even though he can't express in words her mysterious essence. And humankind attains da'at of good and evil, not by intellectualizing about morality and what it is made of – but by experiencing "good and evil" in a raw, direct way.

To summarize, then, in attaining "knowledge" of good and evil, humanity didn't gain a better intellectual understanding of right and wrong. We gained an experiential understanding of these things. We began to know right and wrong from the "inside."

But what, exactly, does that mean? It sounds so abstract. What does it mean to know "good and evil" in a raw, experiential kind of way? I understand what it means to know ice cream experientially and from the inside. I go to Baskin and Robbins, order some "Pralines 'n Cream" on a cone, and eat it – then I've got my "da'at" of ice cream. But what does it mean to know "good and evil" in this way? How does one take "good and evil" inside of oneself?

A closer look at the words "good and evil" (*tov* and *ra*) will help us find answers to our questions.

Right and Wrong from the Inside Out

In chapter one, I alluded to Maimonides' view of our story. In his *Guide to the Perplexed*, Maimonides suggested that Adam and Eve were already aware of right and wrong, in some fashion, before eating from the tree. According to Maimonides, the tree did not give them moral awareness where they had none before. Rather, it *transformed* this awareness from one kind into another. Before eating from the tree, they would not have called virtuous moral choices "good" and vile choices "evil." They would have had a different way of thinking about such things and would have used different words to describe them.

What were these "other words," this original way of looking at things? Well, according to Maimonides, in the pre-Tree world – in the more pristine world – virtuous choices would have been called "true," and reprehensible choices would have been labeled "false." In short, doing the right thing was called "truth"; and doing the wrong thing was called "falsehood."

43

What does Maimonides mean by this? At first glance, his explanation doesn't appear to clarify anything. The word "false" seems to describe "2 + 2 = 5" a lot better than, say, robbing a bank. What does it mean to see morality as a set of choices between "truth and falsehood"? And how does this differ from saying that morality means choosing between "good and evil"?

I don't know for sure, and Maimonides doesn't elaborate all that much on what he means by this. But I have a theory. Let's try thinking of it in these terms:

How are "true" things different from "good" things? When I say something is true, I'm describing objective reality. I'm telling you that something is out there; it's real. And it's real whether I like it or not. If morality is a matter of true and false, this means that making moral choices involves discerning something objective. It involves figuring out what the right thing to do is, what my Maker expects of me – and then trying to align my behavior with that "truth," whether I like it or not.

How, then, do we see virtue differently when we call it "good" rather than "true"? While the word "true" has a core meaning of "real," the word "good" is not quite as objective a term. For example, what else does "good" mean besides "that which is ethically correct"? Its other meaning is: "that which is pleasing." When I say that something is good, what I am really telling you, in a subtle way, is that I approve of it, that it is *desirable*.*

Perhaps, then, Maimonides means the following: The shift from a world of true and false to a world of good and evil was a shift between a world in which I could stand outside my desire to look at choices objectively to a world in which I was confined to

---

* The Torah uses the word "tov" in this way elsewhere. When God saw the light and it was "good", what did that mean? When God said that it was not "good" for man to be alone, what did that mean? Was the light morally good? Was the human morally evil when created without a partner? Neither possibility seems probable. God seems to be saying that the light was *desirable*, and that it was not *desirable* for the human to remain a solitary being. To call something "good" is to approve of it, to say that the thing conforms to my desires.

see things through desire's eyes. In the pre-Tree world, desire did not intrude on the terrain of the intellect. I could discern clearly what God wanted, and my own desires, while powerful, did not cloud that vision. I could see what was "true" and choose it, or disregard it in favor of what I personally wanted to do. If I would choose the latter, I would at least know that I chose my desire over the "true". In the post-Tree world, that clarity is lost. My desire intrudes and becomes an inescapable part of the moral calculus.

As we mentioned earlier, the Tree of Knowledge was deeply associated with desire. It appealed to Eve at all conceivable aesthetic levels, from the most base (taste) to the most profound (mind). If the mysterious Tree of Knowledge was really a tree of desire, then to eat from it was literally to bring desire inside myself; to identify with it. Whereas previously, desire was something outside of my sense of self, something I *possessed*, now I could delude myself into thinking that desire was something I *am*.

Eating from the tree meant a change in equilibrium. In the pre-Tree world, desire was a natural part of humans, but it was recognizable as a mere *part* of who we were, and that part was in equilibrium with the rest of us. It was less likely to blind-side us. In the post-Tree world, that balance can no longer be taken for granted. It becomes a center of gravity; it is always a force to be reckoned with. It becomes a lens through which I view things. No longer do I see a clear world of "true" and "false"; now I see something that is ever so slightly different. I see "good" and "evil" – terms that blur the distinction between virtue and desire.

A World of Broccoli and Pizza

If this still seems a little abstract, let's examine some more commonplace ways in which we use these words, "true" and "false," as well as "good" and "evil." If we pay careful attention to these phrases, we'll hear some echoes of Maimonides' understanding of matters.

To begin with, when we shoot an arrow that hits its mark, we sometimes speak of the arrow having flown "true" to its target. Conversely, the Hebrew word *chet* (sin) signifies "having shot at a target and missed" (e.g. *Judges* 20:16). In effect, when moral decisions are choices between truth and falsehood, it follows that I am trying to "hit a target" when I make these decisions. I am trying to discern my Creator's expectations for me and I am trying to act accordingly. To sin is not primarily about hell-fire and guilt. If it is, that part is only secondary. What it's about primarily is "missing the mark" – failing to align myself with the reality called the Will of my Creator.

Now let's look at the other side of the coin. When a kid pushes away a plate of broccoli and says it's "bad," when he prefers the pizza because it's "good," he is not dispassionately telling you about the quality and nutritional benefits of the food. He's telling you what he likes and what he doesn't like. In a curious way, *he is actually telling you more about himself than he is about the food.*

Consequently, when the Torah speaks of "knowing good and evil," it is using shorthand for a new way of looking at moral choices. Yes, I am still trying to figure out what God wants of me – at least overtly. But there's another factor that can potentially cloud my vision. It's not *only* about what God wants anymore; it's also about what *I* want. Packed inside every moral decision is a little bit of pizza and broccoli. My own desires are now an inescapable part of the picture because now I see each decision through the veil of my desire. I can rise above these desires, but doing so is not always easy.

In the brave new world of good and evil, what I *think* is right and worthwhile is not necessarily what really *is* right and worthwhile. That which is merely "good" – desirable to me – can easily masquerade self-righteously as the "true." When I am looking at life through the filter of my own subjectivity, I may *think* that "x" is what God wants – but perhaps it's really just what *I* want.

Are All Moral Dilemmas Created Equal?

To really get a handle on these ideas, I'd like to take them out of the realm of theory and apply them to real life. Let's try talking about "truth and falsehood" and "good and evil" in the context of some moral dilemmas that you and I might face during the course of our lives.

Try a thought experiment. Below, you'll find a list of several hypothetical moral dilemmas. Take a blank piece of paper. Put a line down the middle and mark one side of the line "Column A" and the other side "Column B." Now see if you can divide the list naturally into two categories. Here are the examples:

- "Is it okay to take a dying man off a respirator?"
- "My elderly mother needs help organizing her house before she moves, but my kid needs me to help him prepare for finals. With whom do I spend the evening?"
- "Should Billy lie to the teacher to protect his friend, Bobby, when the teacher asks him whether Bobby was cheating on his test?"
- It's a dark and rainy night in Manhattan. You throw your trusty Chevy Suburban into reverse and begin to back out of your parking spot, when you hear a sickening thud. You get out of the car to behold, right behind you, a shiny black Lexus convertible – with a badly dented front end. You look around. The street is entirely dark, not a soul to be seen. Do you leave a note or not?

The dilemmas *do* divide naturally into two groups. Three of these dilemmas are real. One of them, though, is fundamentally illusory. Three of the dilemmas exist whether you live in a world of "true and false" or a world of "good and evil." The other exists only in the mixed-up world of "good and evil." In the world of "true and false," it simply evaporates.

Now, which is which?

⁊ Chapter Eight
A Dark and Rainy Night in Manhattan

Okay, let's review. Here are our four dilemmas: the dying man and the respirator; your elderly mother and your kid's homework; Billy and his teacher; and you and your Suburban on a dark Manhattan street.

Well, did you find the impostor?

If you identified the illusory dilemma as the last one – the dark and rainy night in Manhattan – then you and I are on the same page. If you didn't – well, we can still be friends. But in any case, here's my thinking:

The first three dilemmas share a certain, basic quality. They are choices between competing ideals. Each ideal is worthy or noble in its own right, and the dilemma arises only because the two ideals are forced to compete with one another.

For example, take our respirator case: Everyone agrees that prolonging a life is a noble goal, and everyone agrees that improving the quality of a life is also noble, but what happens when you are forced to choose between the two? And consider Billy and Bobby: both honesty and loyalty are worth fighting for. But when each value leads you in a different direction, which one wins out? And so it is with Mom and my son: I have obligations to both these relatives; how do I weigh my competing responsibilities?

All these choices are genuine. There are two boxers in the ring, as it were – two competing values – and the question is: Which boxer wins? Which value is dominant? How does my Creator expect me to act?

But let's turn now to the last case. It's that dark and rainy night in Manhattan, and am I pondering whether to leave that note. Let's identify the competing "ideals" here. Well, first we have honesty. Honesty says leave the note. Okay, now where's the counter-argument? Think carefully…

There is none.

One second. If there's no second ideal, how come it's such a struggle to figure out what to do? It should be a no-brainer. There's only one boxer. Shouldn't he win by forfeit? The answer is: there is indeed another boxer here. But it's not an ideal. It's a boxer named desire.

A Boxer Named Desire

In this last dilemma, the battle is being waged between an ideal – honesty – and *what you would rather do*. The two boxers are simply named: Honesty vs. The Fact that You Don't Want to Leave the Note.

That, of course, is not how your brain presents things to you, though. No, ma'am. Let's listen in on our internal dialogue as you inspect the mangled front end of the Lexus and wrestle with your decision:

> "You know, I really *should* leave that note…. But, one second – before I do that, do I really know for sure that I'm the one who made that dent? I mean, sure I heard a noise when I backed up, but maybe I just ran over a soda can in the gutter or something. And I just *tapped* that Lexus anyway; could I really have made such a big dent?

Boy, I sure would be a sucker if that car was already dented and I left a note. Anyway, what business did he have parking his toy so near my truck? What a fool I'd be to leave *him* a note. Look, it's not like he'll be out any money or anything. Heck, his insurance company will pay. That's what uninsured motorist insurance is *for*, isn't it?"

By the time you're done, you've convinced yourself that it would be positively *virtuous* to walk away. It's Robin Hood vs. the Big Insurance Corporations; it's the little guy vs. the rich and arrogant; it's you vs. your own naiveté – why, you wouldn't be so naive as to think *he* would leave *you* a note if *he* were the one who hit *you*?

But it's all a sham. All those extra "boxers" are phantoms. The real name of the second boxer is simply desire.

Welcome to the world of good and evil.

The Mind-Games of Desire

A fascinating rabbinic teaching echoes this idea.

The Sages state that after a person dies, the Heavenly Court allows him to view his Evil Inclination – his *yetzer hara*, as it were. The Sages go on to say that if the person was righteous in his lifetime, his Evil Inclination appears to him as a mountain, but if he was wicked, it appears to him as a lowly hill. In either case, the person is astonished. The first person is amazed that he managed to surmount the mountain, while the latter is astonished that such a measly hill deterred him.

What do the rabbis mean to say here? At first blush, their teaching is counterintuitive. If anything, one would have expected the reverse. Wasn't the wicked person tormented by the "mountain," by roiling desires he found impossible to subdue? And wasn't the righteous person the one with the tamer sense of personal desire, the mere "hill"?

A friend once suggested to me an interesting explanation. Perhaps the difference between a righteous person and a wicked

51

one is not that one has a greater or more intense yetzer hara than the other; it's that, by and large, the wicked person succumbed to that yetzer hara, whereas the righteous person didn't. That fact alters what each sees when he looks backward: the righteous person sees desire that has not yet been sated, whereas the wicked person sees what desire looks like after one has given into it.

When desire has yet to be sated, it looks like a mountain. Just before you eat the chocolate macadamia fudge torte, you can't imagine anything more delicious. But through the rear view mirror, desire gives a different appearance. Once you've finished off the last crumbs, the mountain is gone, and you see reality for what it really is: the torte tasted good for all of thirty seconds, and now you've got two hours ahead of you in the gym to work it off.

Such are the pitfalls of subjectivity. In the post-Tree world of good and evil, a dilemma is born on the rainy streets of Manhattan. Desire, for all its size and power, dwells unseen within each of us, hiding easily behind "phantom boxers." In this world of subjectivity, evil can get dressed up in pretty clothes – and when it does, it's hard to know the difference between that which is truly virtuous and compelling and that which is merely seductive.

The Beginnings of Desire

Like that rainy night in Manhattan, the choice of whether to eat from the tree or not may have seemed to Adam and Eve like a legitimate dilemma: which voice of God do I listen to – the desire inside me, or the voice that commands me with words?

It seems like a reasonable enough question. And there were good reasons to advocate partaking from this tree of desire. There were good reasons to think it would be right and good and laudable to bring desire into our lives more powerfully than before. After all, the snake is not altogether wrong about instinct and desire constituting the voice of God. Passion *does* come from God, and experiencing it seems to be an essential part of what makes us human. What would it be like to wake up in the morning with no sense of ambition, or to look at a spectacular sunset without a sense of yearning? What if great art seemed humdrum; if romance was wooden and unappealing; if poetry failed to stir our souls? We may well ask if life would still be worth living. To some extent, passion is the very stuff of life.

It's all very reasonable, isn't it? But like that rainy night in Manhattan, there's a sub-text to this dilemma. The intellectual arguments mask another agenda. Even as Adam and Eve stood in the world of true and false, the world of good and evil beckoned to us, and desire began to assert its subtle influence.

ℰ Chapter Nine

The I of the Beholder

The astute reader will notice that when Eve tells the snake what God commanded her not to eat, her paraphrase is different from what God actually commanded. Some of her changes amount to outright inaccuracies; others merely shift the emphasis. For example, Eve identifies the tree she and Adam must avoid as being in the "center of the Garden." However, this wasn't where the forbidden tree was really located. If you look at the verses carefully, you'll find that this is not the only change she makes – there are actually a whole bunch of other ones as well. So, taken as a whole, do these changes suggest a pattern or are they just random misquotations?

Here's a homework assignment: take out those number two pencils and see if you can make a list of the discrepancies. In what ways did Eve miscommunicate God's restriction? When you've got your list together, ask yourself: why did Eve change these details?

Well, it's possible, of course, that Eve was the unfortunate victim of a communications failure. She had not been created yet when the original command to avoid the tree was given, and maybe Adam repeated it inaccurately to her. But maybe something else was afoot. Look carefully and see if you think there is any pattern to the various discrepancies between the original command and Eve's paraphrase of it. I, for one, think such a pattern exists.

Let's examine the verses in question:

God's Original Command:
And God caused to grow from the ground all sorts of trees that were good to look at and good to eat from, and the Tree of Life in the middle of the Garden, and the Tree of Knowledge of Good and Evil (2:10).... And the Lord God commanded Adam saying: "From all the trees you may eat, yes, eat. But from the Tree of Knowledge of Good and Evil, do not eat from it, for on the day you eat from it you will surely die." (2:16–17)

Eve's Paraphrase of that Command:
And the woman said to the serpent: "From the fruit of the trees of the Garden we may eat. But from the fruit of the tree that is in the middle of the Garden, God said not to eat from it and not to touch it lest we die." (3:3–4)

Okay, let's catalogue the differences. What did you come up with? Here's my list:

- **Location of the Forbidden Tree.** Eve says the forbidden tree is in the "middle of the Garden." In fact, according to verse 2:10, it was only the Tree of Life (which was never put off-limits) that was clearly in "the middle of the Garden"; the whereabouts of the Tree of Knowledge are uncertain.*

---

* The verse states that God made "the Tree of Life in the middle of the Garden, and the Tree of Knowledge of Good and Evil." The phrase "in the middle of the Garden" modifies only the first tree, not the second one. If they were both really in the same place, the way to say it would have been: "...the Tree of Life and the Tree of Knowledge in the middle of the Garden."

- **Is Touching Against the Rules?** Eve tells the serpent that she is forbidden even to touch the Tree of Knowledge. In the original command, it is only *eating* from the tree that is prohibited.
- **Fruit vs. Tree.** God speaks of a forbidden tree. Eve speaks of Forbidden Fruit. In practice, perhaps, it's all the same, but the emphasis is certainly different.
- **Is Death a Certainty?** God says that if you eat from the tree, *you shall surely die.* Eve suggests that she and Adam better not eat from the tree "lest" they die. Eve implies a probability of death, not a certainty.
- **When Is Death a Reality?** God says that death becomes a reality *on the day that you eat from the tree.* Eve doesn't mention a time frame.
- **"All" the Trees or Not?** Using repetitive language, God emphasizes that Adam and Eve "may eat, yes, eat" from "all" the trees of the Garden, except the Tree of Knowledge. When talking about the trees she and Adam may eat, Eve removes the emphasized, double language, and also leaves out the word "all." (She uses the more toned-down phrase: "from the trees of the field we may eat…")

Is There a Pattern Here?

What are we to make of all this? Is there any rhyme or reason behind these discrepancies, anything that might explain why Eve made the changes she did in "explaining" the Almighty's prohibition? It seems to me that Eve's changes *do* add up to something.

One might theorize that Eve deliberately distorted God's command or that perhaps she misunderstood the command. I can't conclusively disprove those theories. But to my thinking, a third option seems more likely: namely, that the changes Eve makes were not deliberate at all. Rather, caught off-guard by the serpent and in the heat of the moment, this was just how things looked to her; this was how she wanted to see them.

In other words, the subtle distortions in Eve's words do not, in my opinion, bespeak an intellectual misunderstanding of what God said, but a wishful attempt by the mind to recast God's command in a different light. To put it baldly: if eating from the tree marked the beginning of a more profound role for desire in the life of mankind, then this snapshot of a conversation gives us our first case study in the unseen mechanics by which desire can confound our perception of the way things really are.

Consider this: When we want something that we can't or shouldn't have – but we really want it anyway – what are the things we tell ourselves? How, exactly, does desire begin to work its magic? What do we say to start convincing ourselves that it's really okay for us to have the thing we want? We look at the reality in front of us, and we proceed to delude ourselves by exaggerating certain aspects of it and minimizing others. The game commences, more or less, along the following lines:

- We might begin by exaggerating the extent of the restriction placed upon us, e.g. "even *touching* the tree is forbidden". It's easier to rationalize a wrong if we exaggerate how difficult it is to abide by the rules. How could my parent expect me not to even get near the cookie jar? It's one thing not to eat, but how am I supposed to avoid the entire kitchen?
- Conversely, I might minimize the significance of what I *can* have. In reality, I may "eat, yes, eat" from "*all* the trees in the Garden save one. There are thousands of trees that I am encouraged, maybe even commanded, to partake of. But the mind-games of desire shift the emphasis: sure, we can *eat* from trees, but we can't even *touch* the one in the middle.
- Then we might trivialize the consequences of transgressing. We won't die right away, will we? No, God only meant that today we would become mortal – but death itself won't happen for years and years. Why, of course I should stay away from the tree, but only in case I may eventually die.
- Finally, I might exaggerate the significance of the thing I can't have. It becomes my focus, the center around which

my world starts to revolve. Which tree *is* in the middle of the Garden? For God, the center of the Garden, what occupies His focus, is the Tree of Life – a tree that, surprisingly, was not originally placed off-limits. For Eve, though, the tree she *can't* eat from becomes the center. Desire focuses on the forbidden and magnifies it not because the thing is objectively important, but simply because I can't have it.

In portraying Eve's conversation with the serpent the way it does, the Torah seems to be constructing for us a case study in the dynamics of desire. Here is what it looks like, the text seems to be saying, to struggle with the phantom boxer, the boxer named desire. In subtle ways, things can start to look either bigger or smaller than they really are. The implied warning is clear: don't be too quick to embrace your impeccably constructed arguments about why you really should eat that fruit. First, ask yourself: Am I seeing things the way they really are or just the way I want to see them? Even if I'm not exactly lying to myself about the facts, am I playing with how I emphasize them? Am I exaggerating the importance of some things while minimizing the significance of others?

The Remaining Puzzle Pieces

Now that we understand the extent to which desire played a role in that very first decision of Adam and Eve, it is possible to investigate how the consequences of that choice made themselves felt. How did eating from the tree – even the *struggle over whether* to eat from it – change Adam and Eve? How has it changed *us*? To grapple with these issues, we will need to consider the rest of our story, namely, what transpired after Adam and Eve ate the fruit. So here's what happened next:

- Adam and Eve realize that they are naked and hide from God.
- God asks Adam where he is.

- Adam answers that he is hiding, for he is afraid because he is naked.
- After dismissing Adam and Eve's excuses (she told me to do it; the snake told me to do it), the Almighty imposes various punishments on them, including death, exile, difficulty farming, and pain in childbirth.

Earlier, we pointed out the strangeness of these events. But in reality, the obstacles to understanding are even more troubling than we let on before. Each and every one of these "post-eating-from-Tree" happenings is, I think, perplexing in its own way. Let's go through them one by one and see how:

- *Adam and Eve realize that they are naked and hide from God.* Earlier, in Chapter Four, we discussed how odd this emphasis on nakedness seems. Why, of all things, is *this* the cardinal consequence of eating from a tree bearing knowledge of good and evil? After attaining this knowledge, Adam and Eve do not become aware of a whole new realm of moral dilemmas. Instead, they realize they are naked. Why?
- *God asks Adam where he is.* One second. Do you mean to tell me that the Almighty couldn't find him? Why is God asking a question to which He already knows the answer?
- *Adam answers that he is hiding for he is afraid because he is naked.* Is that how you would put it if you were Adam? First of all, it is strange that Adam singles out his nakedness as the reason he is hiding. If you and I were in Adam's shoes, we probably would have said we were hiding out of shame that we had disobeyed God. But for some reason, in Adam's mind, this sense of shame is trumped by something even more overwhelming – awareness of his own nakedness. Again, we're back to the nakedness theme. Why was this so important to him? Secondly, if you were going to hide because you were naked, what emotion would you pinpoint as the reason you wanted to hide? I don't know about you, but I

would pick either shame or embarrassment. How do we feel when we are naked in public? Embarrassed, I would think. But, strangely, Adam talks about something else. He says he is *afraid* because he is naked. Why, in Adam's mind, does his nakedness inspire not embarrassment but fear?

- **The Almighty imposes various punishments on Adam and Eve.** Okay, let's think about these punishments. We might expect that an omniscient and perfectly just God would impose punishments to fit, in some sense, the crime. There should be some logical correspondence, some tit-for-tat, as it were, between what the people did wrong and the consequences they are made to bear. But what connection is there between punishment and crime in our story? At face value, it seems almost as if the Almighty reached into His celestial grab-bag of consequences and randomly doled out lightning-bolts: "Let's see. Adam? You're the one who works the fields around here. Okay, no more Easy Street for you. From now on, you'll have to work to get harvest out of the land. Eve? Right. You're the one who bears children – let's make that a little tougher. And Snake? You'll crawl on your belly and eat dust, and there will be eternal hatred between your progeny and those of Eve. While we're at it – death to everybody; nobody gets to live forever anymore. Oh, and one last thing: Exile! Everybody out of the pool!"

So we have now laid out the last three pieces of Torah's very elaborate puzzle, the stories of Adam and Eve. These three pieces are: God's strange question, "Where are you"; Adam's intense focus upon and fear of nakedness; and the Almighty's seemingly random imposition of punishments. And I think we are, at last, ready to piece the puzzle together.

Having seen the connection of the Forbidden Fruit story to that of Adam's naming and rejecting the animals; having defined the Forbidden Fruit trial as a challenge to understand why an animal *never* could be our soul-mate; having seen the way human desire in the post-Tree world impedes moral judgment; having seen all this – we are finally in a position, I think, to understand the aftershocks of eating from the tree.

In the final two chapters of Part One, I promise to pull all these threads together. In the meantime, if you'd like to pause and reflect a bit before reading further, you might ask yourself: Are those punishments really as random as they seem? And – given the nature of the tree as we've begun to see it – why might fear of nakedness be exactly the response one might expect from a being who suddenly wakes to find himself inhabiting a radically new world of good and evil?

℘ Chapter Ten

Friedrich Nietzsche and the Disc Jockey

A few years ago, I flipped on the radio while driving in New York City. A disc jockey on one of the music stations was offering to help love-stricken callers sort out their romantic troubles. Listening for a few minutes, I encountered an exchange between the DJ and an earnest young, religious fellow who was explaining why he had chosen to remain sexually abstinent until he was married. The DJ debated with him, and, to my surprise, advanced a *religious* argument – very pious sounding, actually – against the caller. "Tell me," the host began, "are you a normal fellow? Do you have any desires?"

Silence at the other end of the line.

After a suitable pause, the host continued: "Look, why do you think the Lord placed these desires in you if He didn't want you to act upon them?"

The poor fellow hadn't expected to be attacked on religious grounds, and he didn't have much of an answer. As I drove away, my heart went out to the mismatched caller – and it struck me that the primal snake, after all these years, is still alive and well. His argument, despite the passage of time, seems as current now as it ever did. "Even if God *said* don't eat from the tree... so what?"

"God's commands, whatever they may be, are not primary," asserts the snake. "The real voice of the Divine whispers to you from the inside, through the desire and passion that He has instilled in your very being. If your desires were placed inside you by your Creator, then don't you honor Him by doing their bidding?"

Opponents of religion have advanced this rather basic argument throughout history. One such attacker was Friedrich Nietzsche, a nineteenth-century German philosopher, who, fittingly enough, entitled a collection of his essays *Beyond Good and Evil*. In his writings, Nietzsche railed against organized Western religion. He decried the tendency of religion to shun worldly pleasures and delights, to avoid them as if they were something to be feared. Passion, he declared, was the stuff of life itself. If one avoids passion, if one fails to engage it, one has failed the most basic test of humanity. That person has failed to live.

What, really, is the answer to the snake – or, for that matter, the answer to any modern purveyor of his argument? It's all very nice to say that passion is for animals and God's commands are for humans; that animals obey the voice of God inside them and that we obey the voice of God that comes to us through God's commands – but, as humans, are we really ready to consign passion to the dust heap? Desire, when you really think about it, has much to commend it. Passion fires our aesthetic sense. It makes us yearn for beauty, reach out for the spectacular sunset, thrill to the sounds of Yo-Yo Ma's cello. To some extent, Nietzsche was right: our appreciation of these things, at least in part, is what makes us human. The minute I am devoid of desire, the minute I have no ambition left – I have no reason to wake up in the morning. I'm as good as dead.

So where, exactly, was the snake wrong?

To really respond to the snake effectively, we need to re-calibrate our arguments a bit. We need to take one last, long look at desire and see if we really want to dismiss its charms completely. After all, God Himself is passionate, with a Will so powerful that it spontaneously manifests as reality. God desires a universe and, out of nothing, it explodes into being.* What could be wrong, the snake asks, with a little more passion?

Torah and the Spice of Life

A good eighteen centuries ago, the Sages of the Talmud anticipated this line of reasoning, and they put forward a pithy but perplexing aphorism that tries, I think, to respond to it. The aphorism was written in Hebrew; here's how it's usually translated:

> The Holy One, Blessed be He, said to Israel: "My son, I have created the Evil Inclination; and I have created the Torah, its antidote. If you involve yourself in the Torah, you will not be delivered into its hands..." (*Tractate Kiddushin*, 30b).

At first glance, the Sages seem to imply that the Evil Inclination is a problem, a sickness, and the Torah is its solution, the way to get rid of the sickness. But, as is sometimes the case, a lot has been lost in the translation. In the original Hebrew, the Talmud says that the Almighty created the Torah as *tavlin* for the Evil Inclination. Most translations render that word "tavlin" as "antidote" or "salve" ("if you take the antidote...you will not be delivered into its hands"), which seems to fit the context; but, unfortunately, that's not really what tavlin means. If you go to Israel today and walk into a shop and ask for tavlin, they won't direct you to the medicine counter. Instead, they'll walk you over to the spice rack,

---

* It is for this reason, perhaps, that God is known as the ultimate "knower of Good and Evil." Morality, from God's perspective, really *is* a matter of will and desire. It is God's will that we try to align ourselves with. From our perspective, that will is external to us -- hence, we can use the terms "true" and "false" to characterize it. But from God's own perspective, that will is internal. The terms "Good and Evil," which denote categories of desire, are entirely accurate.

and give you a choice of parsley, sage, rosemary or thyme. In Hebrew, tavlin means "spice."

Well, that certainly changes things. If tavlin translates as "spice," what does it mean to say that the Torah is "spice" for the Evil Inclination? What kinds of things do you put spice on?

You put spice on meat; you put spice on food.

Interesting. The Evil Inclination is "meat." What a profoundly different way of looking at things! If you were stuck on a desert island and could be supplied for a year with your choice of either meat or spice, which would your rather have? I'd venture that most of us would opt for the meat. Spice is great, but you can't live on spice. Meat is fuel; meat provides you with the energy to live.

At first blush, it seems surprising, even blasphemous, to see things this way. How dare you say that the Evil Inclination is more "essential," somehow, than Torah! But hold your horses and think a bit about what the Sages are saying. For it's not just the word "tavlin" in this aphorism that defies translation; the term "Evil Inclination" – that thing for which the Torah is meant as tavlin – is just as slippery a concept to grasp.

What, exactly, is this thing named the Evil Inclination? Is it the Dark Side of the Force? Is it some horned devil, complete with pitchfork and bright red suit? Is it some scorned angel with a little too much time on his hands who perches above our left shoulder and whispers bad advice in our ear? When we think about the Evil Inclination, we often envision something darkly metaphysical or faintly childish. But, in real life, what is this thing?

If we exchange the language of the Rabbis for modern, psychological language, we might say that the Evil Inclination is nothing more or less than our passions, our drives, our desires. In fact, we might go a bit further. The Hebrew term for Evil Inclination is *Yetzer Hara*. The root of the word yetzer is *y'tz'r* (to create). If we translate Yetzer Hara quite literally, it would seem to denote – get ready for this – the drive to create, [in] evil [form]. Or, perhaps, more succinctly, Yetzer Hara is creativity gone awry.

Our passions fuel us; they are engines that make us go. Our

drive to create, in particular, is one of the deepest and most fundamental of our passions. Indeed, the creative drive has many outlets: sexuality; artistic endeavor, the yearning to be an inventor, ambition of almost any sort – these are all expressions of creativity at some level. Centuries before Freud and Nietzsche, the Talmud insisted that such forces are essential to our humanity. Without energy, without "meat," you are dead.

But, the Talmud adds, the meat can still use some spice. Let's consider this carefully. What, exactly, does spice do for meat? It gives direction to meat, makes it taste one way rather than another. Without any spice, meat is bland; with the proper spices, it's the dish of kings.

Maybe this explains the Rabbis' insistence that Torah is the tavlin, the spice, for the Evil Inclination. The Torah gives direction to our most basic, most powerful drives. Sexuality, ambition – these things are the highly flammable fuel that combusts inside us and makes us go. It is tempting for religion to look at such raw, daunting forces and to frown upon them, to try to suppress them. The Talmud is saying, though, that the answer to the fearsome power of passion is not to go and take the engines out of our cars, not to renounce "meat" and starve. No, the Torah is designed not to extinguish passion, but to complement it; to provide spice – *direction* – for it; to make desire *taste like something*. The Torah's commands are designed to direct passion toward productive ends, toward worthwhile, even holy, endeavors. Feel your passion, your sexuality, your ambition, the Torah says; don't destroy it. But direct it this way rather than that way. Steer it; don't let it steer you.

The Advent of Imbalance

There was a time when this task of steering was not as difficult as it is now. In the pre-Tree world, passion and intellect were more naturally in balance, so moral clarity was easier to come by. We could make decisions with unfiltered vision, without fear that our desires were distorting the moral landscape, without worrying that our perception of the Creator's Will had been subtly corrupted by our own passionate will to create.

That world changed – *we changed* – when we ate from the Tree of Knowledge. After partaking from this wellspring of desire, Adam and Eve became uneasy. As the locus of our identity shifted toward desire, the delicate balance between passion and intellect became altered. It was as if we were riding in a car, but instead of being seated behind the steering wheel, we found ourselves on the hood, seated atop the engine. In the post-Tree world, Adam and Eve – all of us, really – were left to struggle with this dilemma: how do I direct a powerful, massive engine with a steering wheel I can barely reach?

A Newfound Fear

Immediately after eating from the Tree of Knowledge, Adam hears "the voice of God strolling in the Garden," and he hides, aware that he is naked. Merely hearing God's voice – not anything in particular that God says, but just the awareness of His voice – prompts Adam's anxiety. Having just hearkened to the snake's gambit, having accepted the idea that God *really* speaks to humans through their instinct, their interior voice – at that moment, hearing the voice of God coming from the outside was especially jarring. It was a stark reminder that God does, indeed, speak to humans with words.

Hearing God's voice may have been a stark reminder to Adam that God's expectations go beyond our simply yielding to the engine inside us, letting it take us where it will. And Adam's resulting anxiety takes the form of discomfort over his nakedness. As we mentioned before, the emotion Adam talks about here is not embarrassment – what one would expect from someone who has just realized he is naked – but fear: "I was *afraid* because I was naked, and I hid" (3:10).

Fear is a world away from embarrassment. I become embarrassed when a peer teases me, when I make a gaffe in public. I am fearful, on the other hand, of something I sense that is bigger than I am, of something beyond my control, of something that can crush me. Before he ate from the tree, Adam was well aware that he was naked; he just wasn't *afraid of it*. Sexuality, in the old world, had been just a natural part of life. Why bother with clothes? Now, though, things felt different. Sexuality – the biological manifestation of our drive to create – seemed more overwhelming now. Nakedness – direct, unfiltered confrontation with our own sexuality – is now a source of fear. These powerful passions, newly at the core of my being, may make me godly; but they also can rage beyond control, can't they? How does one steer an engine as fearsome as this?

The Price of Power

After Adam and Eve ate from the tree, God imposed upon them what we described in the preceding chapter as a grab-bag of punishments: death, pain in childbirth, difficulty farming, and the snake having to crawl on his belly and eat dust. But are these punishments really as random as they seem?

Let's start with the snake. Adam and Eve were beguiled by a walking, talking serpent into losing sight of the essential differences between themselves and the animal world. Now, in the aftermath of that failure, God removed that particular source of confusion. No longer would the animal world seem so nearly human. The snake would now crawl on its belly and lose its legs, and, presumably, its ability to speak as well. Moreover, hatred would reign between the children of Eve and the descendants of the snake. Humankind, having once mistaken itself for snakes, will be less likely to do so in the future.

As for the punishments that affect Adam and Eve, are they really punishments at all – or perhaps just consequences? Let's go back to the "engine and steering wheel" analogy. Imagine you have a car built by a supremely competent manufacturer. It works in complete harmony with everything else built by the same manufacturer, and it also works in complete harmony with itself.

If there is no friction between the moving parts of the car, for how long will it last? It lasts forever. Okay. But let's say you take the car and fiddle with the engine, giving it a more powerful profile. You change the car's center of gravity, putting the driver's seat on top of the hood. Well, now you may have more power, but at a price. The harmony is gone. Internally, friction is introduced into the system. The parts, ever so slightly out of balance, grind and eventually wear out. The system will one day break down. Death has become a reality for humankind.

And the "grinding" has other manifestations, too. Childbirth, previously an effortless experience, now becomes a pain-wracked ordeal. Creativity, the creation of new life, is more jarring now. Moreover, we find ourselves slightly out of sync with everything else built by the Manufacturer. In the past, the world of nature effortlessly provided its bounty for Adam. Now, Adam must beat sustenance out of the ground by the sweat of his brow. In the past, we were perfectly in tune with the world around us. Now, when a tsunami stalks silently toward shore, it is the animal world that senses instinctively that something is amiss; it is they that head knowingly for higher ground. Humans remain enclosed in a world of their own, on vacation at the beach, oblivious to the subtle shrieking of the natural world all around them.

There is a final manifestation of this disharmony: we must pick up and go now. As a friend once remarked to me: mankind, no longer at home with himself, finds himself no longer at home in the world created for him either. He suffers exile from the Garden and must make the best of it in new and vaguely foreign terrain.

𝒞 **Chapter Eleven**

History's First Question: Where Are You?

"W here are you?" God calls out to Adam after the latter has eaten the Forbidden Fruit. We asked earlier why the Almighty would ask a question when God already knows the answer. It's time to revisit that issue.

As it turns out, there are two words for "where" in Biblical Hebrew. The more common one is *eiphoh* – but that's not the word the Almighty uses when questing after Adam. He instead invokes the less common word for "where" – *ayeh*.

Is there a difference in meaning between these two words, and, if so, how would one figure out what that difference is? The way to solve such a mystery is not to look at a dictionary – after all, how did the writers of the dictionary figure it out? – but to look at a concordance. A concordance is a nifty little book (actually, it's a nifty *big* book) that lists every occurrence of every word used in the Bible. The point is: if you can trace when and in what contexts the Bible uses the words ayeh and eiphoh, then it becomes possible to connect the dots. The composite picture should point to the unique meaning of each word.

I'll spare you the work of hauling out your concordance. Instead, I'll show you some examples of where each word appears in biblical literature, and let you draw your conclusions. Here are a few representative samples of eiphoh and ayeh:

Some examples of eiphoh:
- *Hagidah na li eiphoh hem ro'im?* – Tell me, please, where are they shepherding? (Joseph, regarding his brothers' whereabouts, Genesis 37:16).
- *Eiphoh likatit hayom?* – "Where did you gather grain today?" (Naomi to Ruth, Ruth 19:2).
- *Eiphoh Shmuel ve'David?* – "Where are Samuel and David?" (King Saul, searching for his nemesis, David, 1 Samuel 19:22).

Some examples of ayeh:
- *Vayigva adam ve'ayo?* – "A man dies, and then where is he?" (Job 14:10).
- *Hineh ha'esh…v'ayeh haseh l'olah?* – "Here's the fire, but where is the lamb for the offering?" (Isaac to Abraham, ascending the mountain on the way to the Binding of Isaac, Genesis 22:7).
- *Ayeh na Eloheihem* – "Where are their gods?" (With reference to idols, Psalms 115:2).
- *Le'imotam yomru ayeh dagan veyayn* – "To their mothers, [starving children] will say: where are grain and wine?" (Lamentations, 2:12).

Well, what do you make of it? See if you can isolate a common denominator in each series of quotes.

Okay, time's up. Ready or not, here's my take on it:

I would submit that eiphoh is a more generic kind of "where" – that is, eiphoh is generally a straightforward request for location. Joseph, for example, simply wants to know where to find his brothers. Naomi wants to know where Ruth has been that day, and Saul is trying to figure out where in the world David is.

Now let's look at ayeh. For the most part, when this word is used you'll find that the questioner is not really interested in finding the location of the thing he is asking about. By way of example: "Where is the grain" the starving children wonder. The children *know* there isn't any grain – if there were, their mothers would have given it to them long ago. Instead, they are exclaiming in agony: "What happened to the grain and wine [we used to have]?" The children are not asking where, in fact, the grain is located; rather, they are crying out in anguish over the bald reality that *it is not here*.

Similarly, "Where is the lamb for the offering?" Isaac asks his father on the way up the mountain. Isaac's point is not that he can't find the lamb. Was it left back at the shack, or maybe in the pen at home? No. His point is that *there is no lamb to be found* when, by rights, there should have been. This apparently innocuous remark by Isaac packs emotional punch, because in it Isaac begins to realize the terrifying truth – that there is no ram here, after all, and that maybe, therefore, *he is the ram*. In sum, when one asks, "Ayeh?" his point is not to find out where something is, but to express wonder that the thing *is not here*, where one would have expected it to be.

This dramatically changes the meaning of God's question to Adam. The Almighty was not asking, "Where are you?" – a simple request for location. Instead he was asking, "Where have you gone? Why are you not here?" As the Sages of the Midrash put it: "'Where are you?' Yesterday, you were with [me and] my da'at. And now, you are with the da'at of the snake." (Midrash Rabbah on Genesis, 19:9)

"Ayeh" is the kind of question you can ask even when you know where something really is. It's a sadder, more mournful word than eiphoh. It happens that ayekah is spelled with precisely the same Hebrew letters (*aleph, yud, kaf, hei*) as 'eichah, the cardinal Hebrew word for "lament." "'Eichah…Look how she sits in solitude!" (Lamentations 1:1), Jeremiah cries, looking upon a destroyed Jerusalem, pining for the bustling crowds who are *no longer there*, who have been exiled to Babylonia. Adam and Eve, too, have been exiled. And perhaps, like Jeremiah's, "'Eichah!" God's outcry, "Ayekah?" is less a question than a lament – a lament at the gulf that now exists between human and Creator:

> I brought Adam into the Garden of Eden and commanded him.
> He transgressed My commands.
> I decreed exile upon him.
> And [upon his departure], I lamented "'eichah/ayekah" ["where have you gone…"].
> And so it was with his children.
> I brought them into the Land of Israel and commanded them.
> They transgressed My commands.
> I decreed exile upon them.
> And [upon their departure], I [once again] lamented "'eichah/ayekah" ["where have you gone…"]
> (Midrash Rabbah on Genesis, 19:9)

Twin Gifts

The story of Adam and Eve in the Garden ends with two final acts of God:

- The Almighty fashions clothes from animal skins for Adam and Eve to replace the more primitive coverings they had made out of leaves.
- After sending Adam and Eve out of the Garden, "lest they eat from the Tree of Life," God stations angels, cherubs with flaming swords, at the entrance to Eden to guard the way back to the Tree of Life.

74

In a poignant way, these two events are closely tied to one another. We noticed earlier that cherubs appear just twice in the entire Five Books of Moses. The only other time we find them is when their likeness adorns the top of the Holy Ark in the Tabernacle, where they guard the Tablets of the Law. Aptly, the Book of Proverbs describes these tablets, or the Torah they represent, as another Tree of Life, "a tree of life to all who grab hold of it" (Proverbs 3:18). Evidently, the same cherubs who keep us away from one Tree of Life grant us access to another one. In a sense, the Torah may be seen as a replacement Tree of Life. Why was a replacement necessary?

After attaining the knowledge of good and evil, humanity became more godly – more passionate, more desirous, more insistently creative. But we were only half-gods. Being truly godly means not just to be passionate, possessed of will, as God is. It means not just to create, as God creates, but to wield wisely the fearsome power of creation. It means to control this power fully, not to be controlled by it. It means keeping passion in balance, realizing that there is a time to create and a time to desist from creating.

After eating from the Tree of Knowledge, after boosting the role of passion in our lives, living eternally was no longer what the Doctor ordered for humankind. A new and different Tree of Life was called for – one that could help restore balance and harmony in the psyche of humankind. The new Tree of Life was designed to help people cope with a new world – a world in which passion could cloud the mind's eye, obscuring what is genuinely right and what is genuinely wrong. The angels that bar human access to one Tree of Life do indeed grant us access to another one. The Torah is a guide to God's Will, a tool that can help people distinguish their own creative impulses from the voice of their Maker. In consuming the fruit of this replacement Tree of Life, in assimilating the viewpoint of the Torah, humanity would be able to sit firmly behind the steering wheel, and we would become fully godly beings, wisely wielding the power of our engines.

75

Stand back, for a moment, and contemplate what happened here. Even as God banished us from Eden, He bequeathed to us the tools we would need to succeed in this new world of our own making.

And now let's talk about God's next act, making clothes for Adam and Eve. In the world that God envisioned for humanity, there would have been no need for clothes; they would have been a superfluity. It was not God's choice that people live in a world where nakedness is something to be feared or avoided. Nevertheless, in this moment of profound disappointment, the Almighty provides Adam and Eve with clothes, giving them the wherewithal to make it in this journey of their own choosing.

Adam's Clothes and Moses's Grave

The Sages of the Midrash (*Tanchuma, Vayishlach #10*) tell us that the Torah begins with an act of kindness and it ends with an act of kindness. The kindness it begins with is God's providing clothing for Adam and Eve. The kindness it ends with, the Rabbis write, is God's act of burying Moses just after he died atop Mt. Nebo, having gazed at the Promised Land but never having set foot there.

In both cases, things had not turned out the way the Master of the Universe might have wished. Adam and Eve disappointed God by eating from the Tree of Knowledge, and, as a result, were evicted from Eden, consigned to die on foreign soil. For his part, Moses disappointed God by striking the rock, and as a result was kept out of the Promised Land, consigned to die in the barren desert. In both instances, people had chosen their own path rather than that of their Creator. And in the wake of both events, people would leave behind the world God had set aside for them for other, unknown shores.

God's reaction in both cases is the same. By burying Moses in the earth when no one else was present to do so, God personally provided Moses the means of transition from this world to another one – a transition which, had God had His way, would not have happened yet. And in providing appropriate clothes for Adam and

Eve, God provided them with a means of transition from Eden to a world they had chosen on their own. Had the Divine Will held sway, this transition would not have happened either.

The stark reality is that beings who possess free will don't always hew to the hopes and expectations of their creators. If this is so with us in respect to God, it is no less so with our own children in respect to us. If we walk away with anything from this closing piece in this study of Adam and Eve in the Garden of Eden, perhaps it should be this: When our children disappoint us, when they make choices we don't approve of; when they exchange the world we have carefully crafted for them for a dubious world of their own making – perhaps we too, after all the consequences have been meted out, after all the words have been said, after all the anguish has been absorbed – perhaps we, too, can provide them with clothes for the journey.

Part II

The World's First Murder: *A Closer Look at Cain and Abel*

৾ Introduction

From Eden to Murder

The story of Cain and Abel seems as if it could have happened at any point in history. One day, two brothers bring offerings to God. God favors one over the other, and the spurned brother murders the favored one.

For most of us, that's all we need to know. Two brothers become rivals, and the rivalry ends in murder. It hardly seems to matter where in the Bible this story appears. It seems a mere point of trivia that Cain and Abel happened to be the children of Adam and Eve, that the story immediately follows the Tree of Knowledge narrative, and that, not so long before, the first humans ate from the Forbidden Fruit and were exiled from Eden. Yes, all that is true – but it all seems incidental. When we read about Cain and Abel, we envision a blank slate, a new chapter in the history of mankind. But slates are rarely as blank as they seem.

In the pages that follow, I will argue to you that the story of Cain and Abel bears the unmistakable imprint of the episode that immediately precedes it, the story of Adam and Eve in the Garden of Eden. The Torah, in a number of subtle and not so subtle ways, goes out of its way to connect these two apparently very different stories. We can debate why the Torah does this, and what

81

it is trying to tell us. But the fact of the connection is, I think, not debatable. For some reason, the story of Cain and Abel is suffused with memories of Eden. That's just the way it is.

You don't have to take my word for any of this. You can see it for yourself. Read the story of Cain and Abel – it's only a few verses long – but don't just read it in a vacuum. Read it side-by-side with the story of Adam and Eve in the Garden. At face value, the stories couldn't seem more different. One deals with talking snakes and Forbidden Fruit; the other deals with a spurned offering and an act of murder. But look a little more closely. Embedded in the verses about Cain and Abel, you will find a curious abundance of parallels to the story of Adam and Eve. Certain key phrases, ideas, or events appear in one story, and then reappear unexpectedly in the next one.

What does it all mean? It's too early to speculate about that. But for now, let's just say this: the story of the Tree of Knowledge is apparently larger than we might first have imagined. It seems to include a "second chapter" – the story of Cain and Abel.

If I'm right about this – and I hope soon to show you that I am – it means that in order to really fathom the significance of our choice to eat of the Tree of Knowledge, we need to examine the immediate aftermath of that choice. We need to look at the story of the world's first murder.

ℰ Chapter One

"So Whose Picture Do You Like Better: Mine or Debbie's?"

There are lots of legitimate questions we can ask about the biblical story of Cain and Abel, yet I'm going to begin this discussion of the episode by raising a question that I consider to be wrong-headed and misleading, a question based on a fundamental misreading of the text. But I'm going to ask it anyway.

Why would I do such a thing? To be perfectly frank, if I thought I could get away with ignoring the question, I would. But I don't think I can. The question is too obvious and too troubling. My guess is that most people who look at the Cain and Abel story are immediately bothered by some shape or form of this question. So we might as well talk about it. If we don't, you'll just think I'm avoiding it.

To observe the question in context, we first need to summarize our story. Here's a quick snapshot of the narrative, followed by my best, devil's-advocate-style rendition of a question I don't really believe in.

Cain and Abel, children of Adam and Eve, each bring offerings to the Lord. The Almighty expresses pleasure with the offering brought by Abel, but not with the one brought by his older brother Cain. Cain becomes very upset. Shortly thereafter, he kills his brother, Abel.

Well, class, that's enough of the story for now. Let's go around the room: Is everyone here happy with this story? I see a lot of shaking heads. Okay. What's wrong with this picture?

To be sure, this story doesn't leave you with that warm, fuzzy feeling inside. What's really jarring, though, is not Cain's act of murder. We know from experience that human beings are capable of doing really bad things. What's really jarring – at least at first glance – is how the Deity chooses to deal with the principals in our story.

Cain brings an offering, and God rejects it in favor Abel's gift. Abel's gift was nicer and prettier, perhaps, than Cain's. The text suggests as much, telling us that Abel brought "from the first of his flocks and from their choicest" (Genesis 4:4), while we hear no such detail about Cain's offering. Still, a little voice inside us asks insistently: Why does God have to reject one and accept the other?

Imagine the scene: You're the mommy, and Bobby and Debbie, your sparkling, wonderful children, are both working on some surprise homemade birthday presents for you. They've got their colored pencils out and are busy creating custom art projects for you. Soon enough, they are done, and each comes over to display his or her work. Debbie walks over first. She proudly shows you her colorful, detailed drawing. She points to the hills, to the sunset, to the little cabin by the stream next to the trees. And she presents the picture to you with a gleam in her eyes: "Here, Mommy… it's your birthday present!"

Next, it's Bobby's turn. Bobby's drawing isn't as detailed. It hardly has much color, and the people who inhabit its landscape are mostly stick figures. Bobby looks at you expectantly, and now it's your turn to speak. What do you do?

Every parent in the world knows what to do. You smile, you look at Bobby, you look at Debbie, and then you say: "My, what beautiful pictures you children have made for me!" And you smother them with love and appreciation.

And what happens if the kids are insistent? "No, Mommy, really!" they squeal. "Tell us which painting you like better!" What do you do then? Well, you know the drill: "I think they are *both wonderful*," you say, as convincingly as possible, as you shoo them off to bed. "They are each beautiful in their own way!"

And what do we think of the parent who doesn't take this approach? Imagine a parent who gently praises Debbie for her meticulously drawn houses, for the carefully chosen hues of green she used for the grass and flowers. But then the parent turns to Bobby and her expression changes as she surveys the choppy lines and scribbles. She exclaims: "Oh, Bobby! What kind of drawing is this? You call these people? They are barely stick figures. And that's a sunset? Please, I can barely see the sun. Come on, Bobby, look at what Debbie made for me. Now there's the way to use your crayons!"

This is not what most of us would call good parenting. It's the kind of thing, we would worry, that's going to put Bobby on the psychiatrist's couch for many years later down the road.

So now let's look at the Cain and Abel story. Both Cain and Abel offer their "presents" to God. And God doesn't smile and say, "My, they're *both so wonderful*!" Instead, God rejects Cain's offering and accepts Abel's.

But I thought parents aren't supposed to do that.

What's going on here? In the story of Cain and Abel, don't we have a classic case of Bobby and Debbie on our hands? What are we to make of the fact that God dismisses our intuitive parenting advice? Is the Bible trying to disabuse us of our modern notions of parenting in favor of something more stern and unforgiving?

85

Bobby and Debbie, Redux

Before giving you my solution to this problem, allow me briefly to make matters worse. Let's get back to Bobby and Debbie, for a minute, and ask: what happens next?

Imagine you were Bobby and Debbie's mother, and when your two children had each presented their respective gifts to you, you had inexplicably disregarded that basic rule of parenting, and had favored Debbie's gift over Bobby's. Now, a half hour later, you walk by Bobby's room and find him weeping softly into his pillow. You ask him what's the matter, and he turns to you and whimpers, "You told me you didn't like my present!" And then comes the kicker, something my child has tried on me one or two times. He says, "*Mommies aren't supposed to say things like that to their kids!*" How would you react to Bobby's plaintive cries?

Instinctively, most parents – even those who had initially favored Debbie's gift – would be unable to resist the sight of a weeping Bobby. Most of us would recognize the error of our ways, would scoop Bobby into our arms and apologize for having turned our back on his gift. You're right, we'd tell him, Mommy loves you, and I'm so sorry for not accepting your gift the way I should have. We'd apologize; we'd tell Bobby we'd had a hard day at work, we weren't paying enough attention; we'd tell him it wouldn't happen again; we'd tell him just about anything in our desperate attempt to make things right.

But that's not how it happens in the Cain and Abel story.

Just after God rejects Cain's offering, and immediately before Cain murders his brother, the Almighty speaks to Cain. But God does not soothingly tell Cain that everything will be just fine, that his offering really was pretty good after all. Instead, God challenges Cain, asking him whether he really has a right to be angry: "Why are you angry and why has your face fallen? Is it not the case that if you do well, then lift up! And if you don't do well, then sin lies crouching at the door…" (4:6–7).

What if the parent who had accepted Debbie's gift but not Bobby's had told the weeping Bobby that if he had done better everything would be just fine; that he should just get over it. Most of us would be ready to pick up the phone and call Social Services. How, then, are we supposed to come to grips with the Almighty's words to Cain?

And now, dear reader, the ball is in your court. I began by saying that I felt the questions I am asking here are not really legitimate. It is my view that the analogy to Bobby and Debbie is faulty and misleading. If you reread the story of Cain and Abel carefully, I think you should be able to spot the flaw; you should be able to see why Bobby and Debbie's sorry circumstance actually has little to do with the story of Cain and Abel.

We'll compare notes in the next chapter.

ॐ Chapter Two

The Enigmatic Genius of Cain

If the Bobby and Debbie scenario (outlined in Chapter One) is an appropriate analogy to the Cain and Abel story, you would have to reach the rather heretical conclusion that the Almighty made a "parenting mistake" in dealing with Cain. This view is in vogue lately among contemporary interpreters. In Bill Moyers's nationally televised discussion of Genesis, for example, a fair number of participants were inclined to take that perspective. But the implications of this view are dramatic and harsh, and we might as well be clear about them.

First, it is a tricky business to ascribe errors in judgment to the Almighty. To do so is probably inconceivable from a theological point of view.* But even if we put traditional theology aside,

---

* It is true, of course, that the Bible itself speaks of God "regretting" having made humankind. But the Bible also speaks of the "outstretched arm" of God, and few of us are willing to concede that God has arms. The Bible sometimes uses anthropomorphism with reference to God, speaking of the Almighty – a Being whose essence we cannot begin to understand – in human terms that we *can* understand. When the Bible does so, though, we are getting just a

from a simple rational perspective it seems preposterous to suggest that the Creator of All lacks basic wisdom about parenting. It is very hard to swallow that the Master of the Universe is less sophisticated about parenting than, say, Dr. Spock, or the latest self-help guru hawking a book on a talk-show.

Evidently, something is rotten with this comparison to Bobby and Debbie. Somehow, God's acceptance of Abel's offering and His rejection of Cain's was *not* like Mommy's preference of Debbie's pretty picture over Bobby's stick figures. Why?

Let's go back to Bobby and Debbie, for a moment, and try to isolate the parenting "sin" that takes place when Mommy tells her kids whose painting she likes better. What, *exactly*, is she doing wrong?

Why My Kids Hate Playing by the Rules of "Boggle"

The great sin, I think, lies in Mommy's stated or implied comparison of Bobby to Debbie. When Bobby and Debbie compete for Mommy's love, when they ask whose painting she likes *better*, that question is a trap. The question, even if asked in the spirit of childhood innocence or playfulness, pits two siblings against each other in a terrible battle for the love and approval of their creator. If the parent buys into this game, if he or she agrees to play referee in this great game of combat, that parent has failed before even saying a word. The terms of play are themselves rotten.

This is not to say that it is wrong for Mommy or Daddy to evaluate their children or to give or withhold approval; what is wrong is to judge one child using the other as a benchmark. The essential point of illegitimacy here is the unfair sense of competi-

---

faint approximation of reality. Whatever God's "arm" means, it doesn't mean a structure composed of bone and flesh that God uses to eat his dinner. And whatever God's "regret" implies, it doesn't mean the prosaic emotion that afflicts us mortals when we realize we've made a boo-boo. The regret of an all-powerful, all-knowing Being is of a different nature altogether, and its true meaning is shrouded in mystery.

tion, the fact that Debbie becomes the measuring stick by which Bobby is judged, the fact that, as a result, neither Bobby's nor Debbie's acts are really seen as valuable in and of themselves, but only insofar as they measure up to or outshine the accomplishments of the other.

There is a game we sometimes play around the table with our kids. It is a word game called "Boggle." In Boggle, each player looks at a grid of letters and has sixty seconds to identify a list of words that emerge from contiguous letters. There is a rule in Boggle that all my kids universally hate. The rule is that if all the players around the table have discovered the same word, no one gets any credit for it. Every player is just supposed to strike those words from their list; they simply don't count.

Now, from a strictly utilitarian point of view, this rule makes a lot of sense. It simplifies the process of keeping score. But it's the message behind the rule, I think, which draws my kids' ire. The message is: "What you found, what you discovered, doesn't count, if your brother Bobby found it too." Your acts don't have inherent worth or value; they can be canceled out by what your siblings do or don't do.

Was Cain Compared to Abel – or to Himself?

Now let's look at the story of Cain and Abel, this time reading it more carefully than before. Ask yourself: *why* did God reject the offering brought by Cain? Let's read the text and see what it tells us about each brother's offering:

> And in the process of time it happened that Cain brought of the fruit of the ground an offering to the Lord. And Abel, he also brought of the first of his flocks and of their choicest ones. And the Lord turned to the offering of Abel, but to Cain and his offering he did not turn. (Genesis 4:3–5)

Look closely. Is the Almighty playing with Boggle's rules, or not? The text *does* say that Abel took "from the first of his flocks and from their choicest ones," whereas we hear no such detail about Cain, only that he brought "of the fruit of the ground." The implication is that Abel offered the *best* of what he had, whereas Cain simply offered *some* of what he had – average produce, produce that didn't stand out as either the best or worst of what he had.

But ask yourself this deceptively simple question: when measured against each other, which offering was of higher quality? You might be tempted to answer that it was Abel's – Abel brought the better stuff. But the real answer is: we simply don't know.

Nowhere is there evidence suggesting Abel's offering was worth more or was superior to Cain's. We know that Abel offered *the best* of what he had, whereas Cain offered simply *some* of what he had, but we don't know how one offering stacked up against the other. It is entirely possible that Cain's offering was worth more, that his average stuff was higher quality than the best of what Abel had. We just don't know. The bottom line is: Abel brought the best he could; Cain didn't. Each brother is compared not to the other, but to himself. What he *did* is compared to *what he could have done.*

If Bobby and Debbie both show up with pictures for Mommy's birthday, and Mommy discerns that Debbie did the best she could with the picture, while Bobby's picture looks like something he threw together while watching cartoons on TV, it is entirely appropriate for Mommy to note this fact. It doesn't matter that Bobby might be the better artist, that at an art auction Bobby's absent-minded doodles might fetch a greater price than Debbie's carefully crafted sunset. All this is irrelevant. If Mommy senses that, relative to his own talents, Bobby presented her with something nondescript, she is entitled to voice her opinion.

Which brings us to a very important question: Why did Cain do what he did? If you're going to bring an offering to God, wouldn't you bring the good stuff? What exactly was Cain thinking?

The Enigmatic Genius of Cain

In our mind's eye, I think we often construct an inaccurate portrait of Cain. One tends to think of Cain as a grudging imitator of Abel. We imagine, perhaps, that Cain saw his brother bringing an offering to God, and, not wanting to be outdone, Cain figured he would play along. His heart wasn't really in it, though, so he didn't bring the best of what he had.

But in reality it didn't happen like that. It wasn't Abel who had the brainstorm to bring the first offering – it was Cain. Cain was the originator, the first person in the history of the world to bring an offering to God.

It seems strange to say so, but this fact alone qualifies Cain as a kind of spiritual genius. Whatever else one may think of the notion of offerings to God, one thing is sure – the idea has stood the test of time. A wheel may seem simple and obvious, but its inventor is a genius. Cain, too, was a kind of genius – he began something, and hundreds of religions representing millions and millions of people have followed suit. All in all, this makes Cain a much harder figure to peg.

How are we to understand a man who introduces the idea of offerings to the world, but then, when he actually brings this first of all offerings, brings nondescript, average produce? If you are an innovator, you are not likely to be the kind of person who does things halfway. Why does Cain, the bold inventor of offerings, not bring the best of what he has to God? Cain's genius is enigmatic, indeed.

This is the central challenge the Bible presents in this tale: how are we to decipher Cain? Like it or not, the story is not really about Abel. He just gets killed, and we know nothing more of him. It is Cain whose legacy endures. It is Cain whose acts and thoughts are the focus of our story. It is Cain the Torah is asking us to try to understand.

A Question of Placement

Our quest to make sense of this story can be helped, I think, by

93

pulling back our zoom lens and getting a broad, landscape view of our narrative. I'd like to get back to an issue I raised in the Introduction to Part Two, namely: is there any meaning in the fact that the Cain and Abel story appears in the Bible precisely where it does?

On one level, there doesn't seem to be anything remarkable about the placement of the story. It comes right after the episode of Adam and Eve in the Garden, presumably because that's when it took place. The narrative appears here because that is its rightful place in the chronology of events, right?

Well, yes, but sometimes chronology isn't everything. As we saw in Part One, the links between juxtaposed biblical stories often run far deeper than the incidental fact that one story happened right before or after another. Stories appearing next to each other in the Bible often shed light on each other in surprising ways.

Is that the case with the Cain and Abel narrative? Is the story of humankind's first murder connected in any essential, meaningful way to the events that preceded it, namely, Adam and Eve's experience with the Forbidden Fruit, and their subsequent banishment from Eden?

Look at these stories again, and see if you can find any clues. Then turn the page, and we'll talk.

ৈ Chapter Three
Echoes of Eden

The story of Cain and Abel is suffused with the memories of Eden. Embedded in the verses of the world's first murder are abundant parallels to the story of the Forbidden Fruit. Certain key phrases, ideas, or events appear in one story, then reappear unexpectedly in the next one. Let's examine some of these links.

A "Missing Persons" Alert

Immediately after Cain kills his brother, God addresses Cain with a question: "Where is Abel, your brother?" (Genesis 4:9).

One second, that part seems familiar, doesn't it? In the Eden story, there is a question like that, too, no? After Adam commits *his* great misdeed – after he eats from the Forbidden Fruit – God addresses him with a question as well: "Where are you?" (Genesis 3:9).

In each story, God quests after a missing person. And the quest itself is of a very particular kind. It takes the form of the question *"ayeh" – where is he?"* In our discussion of Adam and Eve in Part One, we indicated that there are two Hebrew words for "where". The more common one is eiphoh; the less common is ayeh. In each of these two stories, it is the less common, ayeh form of "where" that God uses.

What's the difference between eiphoh and ayeh? As we discussed earlier, eiphoh seems to be a more generic "where," a basic request for location. Ayeh, on the other hand, is used when the questioner is less interested in where something is than in why *it is not here*, where it ought to be. In Eden, it is the ayeh question that is asked: Not where is Adam, but *where has Adam gone? What happened to him?* So, too, in the story of Cain and Abel, the ayeh question is asked: Not where is Abel, but *where has Abel gone? What happened to him?*

Hide and Seek

Let's go on. How do Adam and Cain each respond to the ayeh question from the Almighty? Adam, overcome with the consequences of his deed, aware of his newfound vulnerability, states that he has been hiding from God: "I heard your voice in the Garden and was afraid because I was naked, and I hid" (3:10).

At first glance, we don't find anything comparable in the Cain story. We do not find Cain trying to hide behind any bushes, nor does Cain complain about being naked. But listen carefully to the following two verses, and see if you can't discern in them the echo of Adam's words:

> And Cain said to God: "My sin is greater than I can bear. Here you have cast me away today from upon the face of the earth and from your face I will hide; I will be a wanderer in the land, and everyone that finds me will kill me..." (Genesis 4:13–14)

Just as Adam speaks of hiding from God, so, too, does Cain. Tucked into Cain's response to God is a curious premonition that he is destined to spend his life hiding from the Almighty: "...and from your face I will hide..." Adam hides in the past tense: at a particular point in time, he hides from God and then explains to the Almighty that he has done so. Cain hides in the future tense: banished to a life of exile, Cain intuits that he will spend his days in a continual state of isolation from his Maker.

No Place Like Home

The parallels continue. Having eaten of the Forbidden Fruit, Adam is told that he and Eve must leave Eden, never to return. They are exiled from the only home they know. Cain, too, must leave home in consequence of his actions: "…a wanderer shall you be throughout the land…" (Genesis 4:12). Adam and Eve, in the wake of their sin, are forced to leave Eden and make a home for themselves elsewhere. Cain, in the aftermath of his sin, cannot find a home anywhere.

To Be Cursed from the Ground

In addition to perpetual exile, the Almighty imposes one more curse upon Cain. Henceforth, Cain's efforts at farming will meet with frustration: "And now: Cursed are you from the ground that has opened its maw to take your brother's blood from your hand. When you work the land, it will not continue to give its strength to you…" (Genesis 4:11–12).

Once again, we are transported back to the Eden story. It was not just Cain who experienced difficulty farming at the behest of the Almighty. Adam, too, in the aftermath of eating from the Tree of Knowledge, heard very similar words from God: "Cursed is the land on your account; in toil will you eat from it all the days of your life. Thorns and thistles will it grow for you, and you will eat the grass of the field. By the sweat of your brow will you eat bread…" (Genesis 3:17–19).

Adam is told that he must wrest his sustenance from the ground; Cain is told that, although he works the land, it will no longer give its strength to him.

A Growing Intensity

So now, let's add it all up:

97

- Both Adam and Cain hear the Divine question: "Ayeh?"
- Both Adam and Cain express fear and hide from God.
- Both Adam and Cain suffer exile.
- Both Adam and Cain are condemned to experience difficulty farming.

Clearly, the Cain story is filled with the imagery, language, and ideas that animate Adam and Eve's banishment from the Garden. Somehow, Adam and Eve's experience in Eden is gone but not forgotten. Somehow, the silent presence – or absence – of the Garden continues to dominate and define the lives of those who have long since left its confines.

The mystery behind these connections extends still deeper. There is more to the four parallels than immediately meets the eye. The elements are not simply *repeated* from story to story; rather, each element expresses itself a little differently when it reappears a second time. Let's look for the pattern:

- **"Ayeh."** In the Garden of Eden, God seeks the whereabouts of a temporarily missing person (Adam). In the story of Cain and Abel, the person He seeks (Abel) is gone for good.
- **Hiding.** In the immediate aftermath of his sin, Adam hides from God momentarily. Cain, on the other hand, intuits that he will spend his life hiding from God; that he will do so perpetually in the indefinite future.
- **Difficulty Farming.** Adam will have to wrest bread out of the ground "by the sweat of his brow." He will have to work to till the land; he will have to fight weeds and thorns – but at the end of the day, he will have his bread. Cain, on the other hand, is told that even if he works the land with mighty toil, "it will not continue to give its strength to you." Cain will experience a fundamental loss of agricultural potential. The land simply won't produce anymore what it once did.
- **Exile.** Before eating from the tree, Adam and Eve called

Paradise their home. Now, they will have to leave these idyllic environs to build a new home elsewhere. Cain, too, suffers exile, but of a different magnitude altogether: No matter where he seeks to build his home, the land will not graciously offer him shelter. Not only must he leave home, but he will never be able to call any place his home.

In each of these four examples, the response to Cain's wrongdoing is a more intense version of Adam's experience. Whatever happened in the wake of Adam & Eve's eating from the Forbidden Fruit, happens again after Cain murders Abel – but when it occurs a second time, it occurs with greater force and impact. Each of these parallel elements intensifies in the story of Cain. What is the Bible telling us here?

A Working Hypothesis

At the very least, it is apparent that these stories are connected. But the fact that the consequences *intensify* from story to story suggests more than merely a casual connection between the narratives. It suggests that there is a progression from one incident to the next. It suggests that failure in Eden *sets the stage* for Cain and Abel. It is as if you could place the two stories – Adam and Eve in the Garden, and Cain and Abel – on successive steps of a ladder. When you face the challenge of the Garden and fail, that sets up a new challenge – a challenge that is a next step on the same ladder. The consequences for failure in the second challenge are rightfully the same as they were at the earlier level, only they are felt more intensely.

What does all this actually mean? Why would a story about eating from the Tree of Knowledge of Good and Evil set up a story about sibling rivalry, spurned sacrifices, and murder? If the Cain and Abel story is about offering the wrong thing to the Almighty; if it is about the inability of two brothers to get along; if it is about the terrible fruits of jealousy – what does this have to do with the choice to eat from a mysterious tree that God put off-limits? How, *really*, are the challenges faced in one story in any way similar to the challenges faced in the other?

Somehow, the questions Cain faces – what kind of offering to bring to God, whether to invite Abel for a menacing stroll in the field – are born of Adam's decision to eat the Forbidden Fruit. Our challenge will be to figure out how this is so.

ℰ Chapter Four
Blood on the Ground

I f it were up to you to sentence the first murderer in the history of the world, what punishment would you impose? You'd probably try to come up with something that fits the crime. Perhaps Cain should himself be killed to avenge his brother's blood. If you were in a less punitive frame of mind, you might argue that Cain should be forced to experience something that teaches him about the horrors of murder. Or, if you were really in a lenient mood, you might opt for a rigorous community-service assignment: maybe Cain should be required to contribute in some fundamental way to the building of human society.

But God does not choose any of these options. Here is the Almighty's response:

> "And now: Cursed are you from the ground that has opened its mouth to take the blood of your brother from your hand. When you work the ground, it will no longer give its strength to you; a wanderer shall you be throughout the land." (Genesis 4:11:12)

God declares that Cain shall be "cursed from the earth," that he shall experience difficulty farming and be a wanderer. But what does any of this have to do with Cain's act of killing his brother?

The verse itself supplies an answer. It says that the earth has "opened its mouth to accept" Abel's blood, and for this reason, Cain shall experience a curse with respect to that same earth. But there's something less than satisfying, at least at face value, with this explanation. One can't help feeling that the ground's role is rather incidental here. It happened that Abel's blood fell on the ground and soaked into the earth, but that doesn't describe the essential heinousness of the crime, does it? If Abel's blood had fallen on the kitchen floor instead, would Cain have been cursed through linoleum tiles?

A Focus on the Ground

A closer look at things reveals something astir in this text. For some reason, the "earth" is very important in these verses. The ground is not an incidental part of Cain's punishment; it is the essential core of it. Everything that happens to him is phrased in terms of the ground. First, Cain is told that he will be cursed "from *the land*"; next, that when he works *the land, the land* will no longer give its strength to him; and, finally, that he will be a wanderer throughout *the land*. The Torah's focus on land here is relentless, and Cain's anguish in the face of all this is palpable: "My sin is greater than I can bear... here you have cast me away from the face of the earth..."

Why, of all things, is Cain's relationship to the ground targeted by the Almighty in response to his act of fratricide? And why is Cain so deeply affected by this targeting?

Cain's Name and His Profession

A clue lurks in two things we learn about Cain the moment we are introduced to him. The text tells us his name and his profession: he is called Cain, and he chooses to be a farmer. Curiously, these two facts are related.

102

One might think of names as essentially arbitrary tags. But particularly in the Bible, names are often important clues. When we name our children, we try to embody our hopes for them; we try to sum up who we think they are, or hope they will be. All the more so with Cain; for, in fact, Cain was never actually named Cain. He just *was* Cain.

"And Eve conceived and bore Cain…" (Genesis 4:1).

Other children in the Bible – Ishmael, Moses and Samuel, for example – are *given* names by parents or by others. But not Cain. In his case, the association between name and identity runs even deeper. He is not someone merely named Cain; he *is* Cain; he embodies the word. But what does the name mean?

In Hebrew, Cain's name is *kayin*. The context suggests that the name derives from the word *kanah*, which means "acquire." Cain the Farmer works the earth. And Cain the Acquirer seeks to ground himself in possessions. For both, land – ground – is indispensable.

Why Real Estate Is So Real

It is no coincidence that people call land "real estate." It is called that because it is the most "real" thing we can have. By comparison, everything else is transitory. Everything else comes and goes. Even *we* come and go. We die and are gone. But not land. Land sticks around. And having it makes us feel real; it makes us feel anchored to something that lasts.

Cain the Acquirer has a special relationship to land. It is here that we come to an interesting difference between Cain and Abel. While "Cain" comes from the word "kanah" (acquire), the name "Abel" comes from the very opposite. In Hebrew, Abel is *hevel*, which means, of all things, "breath", or, more precisely, the steam that escapes one's mouth on a cold winter's day.

Hevel is a word that appears elsewhere in the Bible. Its most common string of occurrences is in the Book of Ecclesiastes. Hevel, in fact, is the first word in that book: "Vanity of vanities, all is vanity," says Solomon in Ecclesiastes. Except what he's really saying is *"hevel havalim."* Everything is hevel, everything is "breath."

What does it mean to say everything is breath? It goes to the very heart of the Book of Ecclesiastes. In that book, Solomon, one of the richest, most successful men ever to live, reveals his anguish – an anguish that is, ironically, the stepchild of his success. His distress comes from the realization that his achievements will not, cannot, last. Everything, Solomon declares, is like breath. It all dissipates. It all ends with death. At the great door to the next world, you have to leave everything behind you.

It is not just that you can't take your wealth or possessions with you. That would be bad enough. But the successful man wants more than wealth. He wants to make a difference. He wants to leave his mark on the world. Here, too, he is frustrated by the problem of "breath." All the rivers flow to the sea, Solomon observes, but it doesn't seem to matter. The sea is still not full. We try to make a lasting impression; but, in the end, only one thing lasts: "One generation comes, one generation goes, but the land lasts forever" (Ecclesiastes 1:4).

The earth itself outlasts us. It alone, in the world we inhabit, has the aura of permanence. And by clinging to the earth, we achieve a measure of solace against the great terror of hevel, of breath.

Hevel – Abel/breath – dies. Hevel is unattached and transitory; he chooses to herd sheep. But Cain the Acquirer attaches himself to the ground – he becomes a worker of the earth – and relentlessly seeks to share in its permanence.

Triangular Consequence

And now we come back to the consequences for Cain's act of murder. If you look carefully, I think you'll find that the three elements of Cain's punishment are closely related. They form a kind of "triangle," if you will. The top of the triangle states a principle, and the two "sides" express how the principle plays out.

The top of the triangle is the general, opening statement that

Cain will be "cursed from the land"* – that Cain will be separated from the ground. And what are the consequences of this separation between Cain and the earth? For that, we look to the two "sides" of the triangle. The effects are that Cain becomes a wanderer, and he experiences difficulty farming.

We human beings get two basic things from the ground. First, the ground "grounds" us; it gives us a place to be. Secondly, the ground nourishes us. The soil provides us with the fruits and vegetation that we cultivate through agriculture.

Cain related to both these aspects of the ground. He cultivated the earth in an effort to partake of its nourishment, and he was the "acquirer," a man seeking "grounding." Now, in both these respects, Cain becomes "distant" – cursed – from the ground.

First off, the ground will no longer give him a place to be. He will become a wanderer, unable to settle down anywhere.† But it

---

* Yes, the syntax is awkward, but in Hebrew that's exactly what the text says: that Cain will be cursed *from* the ground. The strange phrase can either mean that the ground is the source of Cain's curse (the one doing the cursing, as it were), or that the effect of the curse is to separate Cain *from* the land. Either way, the sense is that a rupture has occurred between Cain and the ground. The earth is being portrayed in strangely sentient and personal terms, and the implication is that something has gone wrong with Cain's relationship with this being, the earth.

† Interestingly, the end of the story tells us that Cain settles in the land of Nod and builds a city, which he names after his son. At first glance, Cain seems to have succeeded in subverting his decree of exile, but the place he has "settled" in is not really a place; its name is the Land of Nod, a Hebrew term that means "the Land of Wandering". And, as the classic commentator Nachmanides notes, the Torah speaks of Cain's urban construction project – his building of a city – in the *present tense*. The text doesn't say, as you might expect, that Cain *built* a city and dedicated it to his son, but rather that "*Cain **was building** a city and dedicated it to his son...*"

According to Nachmanides, the present tense indicates that Cain never finished the project. He was *perpetually* "building", starting at one point, then stopping, then starting again, always dreaming the dream but never able to see the project through to completion. Cain desperately seeks to ground himself – to make a home for himself, or to build a whole city full of homes.

is not just in the sense of "home and hearth" that Cain is rootless. Cain's lack of roots expresses itself quite literally in an inability to cultivate roots, an inability to succeed in the great enterprise of agriculture. The second leg of Cain's triangle is that the ground will no longer give him its strength; it will no longer provide him with the bounty he had sought through farming.

A Divorce from the Earth

For Cain, the impact of this triangle of consequences seems less economic than personal. He has been distanced from something that really matters. This, at least, is how Cain himself seems to see it: "My sin is greater than I can bear. Here, you have cast me away today from upon the face of the earth, and from Your Face I will hide."

When Cain speaks of being "cast away" from the earth, the Hebrew word is *gerashti*. Speakers of Hebrew will be familiar with the word. Its other meaning is "divorce," the termination of the marriage bond between a man and woman. In Cain's eyes, he has been rejected, separated – *divorced*, even – from the earth. This painful distance expresses itself in the two fundamental ways the earth takes care of us, in its ability to give us a home and in its capacity to nourish us. In both these ways, Cain finds himself at odds with the earth.

And so, we begin to see how the twin portraits of Cain the Farmer and Cain the Acquirer merge into a fuller portrait of Cain and the consequences that befall him. But we have so far glimpsed just a part of an even larger, more expansive picture. For in fact, the links between Cain the Farmer and Cain the Acquirer go far deeper than this. Indeed, if we look carefully at these two aspects of Cain, we will discern the answers to the two fundamental questions we raised at the outset: Why would Cain, a man bold enough

But he is a wanderer. The harder he tries, the more the dream evades him. He is truly rootless, condemned in every sense of the word to a life of complete transience.

to bring the first recorded offering to God in the history of man-kind, choose to give merely average produce as his gift? And why is the story of Cain so eerily reminiscent of the story of Eden?

੬ Chapter Five
Living the Dream of Eve

Let's turn our attention back to the question we first raised in chapter two: Why would Cain, the first person ever recorded to present an offering to God, choose to bring merely average produce in that offering? Why would an innovator choose to do something half-way?

It's hard to know where to turn for clues. The text itself is very sparse. It doesn't say much about Cain before he goes and offers his offering, before he goes and kills his brother. But it does tell us something. We are told Cain's name and his profession. He is a man called Cain, and he chooses to become a farmer, a worker of the land.

As we discussed earlier, both Cain's name and his profession revolve around "land." But I also indicated that there is an even deeper connection between these two facts. If we can succeed in illuminating this connection, it will help us understand what motivates Cain and why he makes the choices he does.

Cain and Eve

The truth is: we know more about Cain's name than just what it was. We also know how he got it. The text clues us in to the words

109

his mother spoke when she was giving birth to him: "[Eve] conceived and bore Cain. And she said: 'I have acquired a man with God'" (Genesis 4:1).

At first glance, Eve's exclamation seems a trivial piece of information, a nice bit of color commentary to be sure, but seemingly unrelated to a larger story that revolves around offerings, jealousy, and death. Surely, though, the Bible is not reporting mere delivery-room banter here. Eve has said something significant. She has said something that matters to our story. Otherwise we wouldn't be hearing about it. But *why* does it matter?

To see the true significance of her words, the first thing we have to do is gently untether ourselves from the English translations. In English, the verse seems to be relaying two disjointed facts, that Eve had a child named Cain, and just happened to utter such and such a phrase. But the Hebrew tells an entirely different story. Listen to the Hebrew for a moment: "...*vateled et* **kayin,** *vatomar: 'kaniti ish et HaShem.'*"

After giving birth to *kayin*, Eve says *kaniti ish et HaShem*. The name Cain – Hebrew 'kayin – is a paraphrase of the words his mother utters when giving birth to him: "I have 'acquired' [kaniti] a man with God."* Cain's name evidently derives from what his mother had to say when birthing him. It behooves us, then, to see if we can understand what she was trying to say.

The Wonder of it All

"I have acquired a man with God." The phrase, at first, seems strange and cryptic. We might understand it, though, if we consider what *we* might have said had we found ourselves in Eve's position.

Eve had just gone through an event we've grown used to calling "childbirth". Yet Eve didn't just experience any run-of-the-mill act of childbirth, if indeed one can call any birth "ordinary". She

---

* Kayin is actually an anagram formed from the first three letters of kaniti. *Kuf, Nun, Yud* is transposed to become *Kuf, Yud, Nun.*

was a principal in the first human birth in the history of mankind.

As a father, I am obviously limited in my ability to talk from experience about the act of giving birth. But if I can extrapolate anything from the way my wife remembers the moments she gave birth to our children, I can tell you that a woman experiences this event as a supreme wonder. Yes, the experience is usually painful beyond words; but, at least in my wife's case, the enormity of the pain was mixed with her palpable sense of awe at what was happening. She was experiencing the creation of a new being, literally, from the inside out. She was not a passive bystander in that experience. She was herself a partner in a new, bold, visceral act of creation.

A partner with whom? Well, the obvious answer would be "me", the father. But I'm actually not referring to myself here. It is humbling to say so, but the man's role in all this is rather fleeting, and a woman in the throes of childbirth can easily overlook it. At least Eve apparently did. The partner I am referring to is another Being – the Force, as it were, behind the womb.

The womb is an astounding organ. Hundreds of years of medical technology and billions of dollars in research have failed to replicate it. We have learned how to conceive fetuses in test tubes, but we cannot grow them into children without a womb. A child that leaves this special place more than a few months before its time simply has no chance of surviving. There is no such thing as an artificial womb.

The uniqueness of the womb is a bit surprising, since at first glance it doesn't seem to do all that much. But it is precisely the womb's quietness – its ability to be still, to "listen" and gently respond – that is its genius. Modern science has revealed the womb to be an exquisitely responsive organ, a vehicle that senses its occupant's every need and tailors itself to accommodate that need. It provides a precise and ever-changing balance of nutrients; it maintains perfectly calibrated PH levels; it discreetly disposes of toxins; it provides the right enzymes and antibodies at precisely the right time and in just the right doses. The biochemistry of the womb is complex beyond imagining. A womb is not the work of humans. We could never have devised it. Through her womb, a woman encounters not just her child, but the Almighty Himself. In her own creativity, she experiences the nearness of the Creator of All.

If every woman who goes through childbirth is at least dimly aware of this mystery – if every woman, at least to some extent, senses the "science-fiction-like" quality of childbirth – think how Eve must have felt. What she went through didn't just *seem* utterly new and unprecedented. It *was* utterly new and unprecedented. This was the first human birth in history. *No one* had ever been through this before. She must have experienced herself as being part of a miracle beyond imagining.

Eve saw clearly the breathtaking implications of her experience. Until now, there was only one Creator in the world. He alone was responsible for the existence of everything, from moon and stars to grass and trees, from elephants and zebras to sky and earth. But all that changed now. Now, God had taken a partner and had ushered her into the great secret of Creation. That partner was Eve.

"I have acquired a man with God!" (Genesis 4:1), Eve cries exultantly. *Look what God and I have done. We have created this little man together!*

Moshe and the Tomato Plant

We are now, I think, in a position to see a deeper, more vibrant, link between Cain's name and his profession. It is not just that both of these revolve around land. Rather, both Cain's name and his profession speak to one of the most intoxicating pursuits that we as human beings can hope to be engaged in. Each speaks to the possibility of becoming a partner with God in the act of creation.

Think about it – what's the big deal in being a farmer? Yes, you get the obvious utilitarian benefits. You can get food by raising crops. Plus, you remain connected to the land, you remain "grounded", as we suggested before. But there is something more. There is great joy to be found in farming, a joy that many of us moderns have become too jaded to see.

In our world, we are used to seeing fruits and vegetables as mere things. We either consume them at our table (if we care about nutrition), or we trade them on the commodities exchange (if we care about our pocketbook). Tomatoes, as any good city-child will tell you, come from the supermarket, not from the ground. But there is another story that fruits and vegetables tell, and it is a story that can leave us awestruck. We can still access that wonder if we try.

I personally discovered that wonder through my child. It sounds ridiculous to say it now, but when my son, Moshe, was maybe three or four years old, I used to regale him at bedtime with stories about him and his imaginary friend, his ceiling fan. Yes, "Moshe and the Fan" had all sorts of adventures together. There were the usual cops and robbers tales, of course, but the story that really captured my son's attention was the one about the tomato garden. It goes like this:

Once upon a time, Moshe took some little seeds from a pouch and sprinkled them on the ground. "What are you doing?" asked his trusty fan. Moshe explained that he was planting tomatoes. "Don't be ridiculous," said the fan, "those aren't tomatoes. Those are little tiny crumbs. And why are you wasting them by putting them on the ground?" Moshe told his fan to be patient, and went to fetch his shovel. "Why are you burying those things?" shrieked the fan, "now you're *really* ruining them!" But the fan had seen nothing yet. Soon, Moshe started dumping water on the ground with his bucket. "You're drowning everything and just making a muddy mess," said the fan, "let's go home."

But Moshe, so the story goes, would not be deterred. He patiently explained to his friend that he was planting seeds; that these would soon grow into green, leafy plants; and that these plants, in turn, would soon give him lots of tomatoes. The fan couldn't contain his laughter. He thought Moshe had lost his mind.

Every day, Moshe would drag his chortling fan back to the same spot in the backyard and would look to see if his plants were growing. And every day, the fan would make fun of him. "This planting thing is ridiculous," chided the fan. "When are you going to outgrow these childhood games?"

Well, you know what happens next. One day, as Moshe was dejectedly walking back from his plot of land, he turned around for one last peek. "There!" he shouted. "Do you see that little green shoot? That's my plant!" And sure enough, there it was. The tomato plant continued to grow, and suffice it to say that by the time bedtime was over a vindicated Moshe and his no-longer-skeptical fan were delighting in a feast of newly-harvested tomatoes.

Every time I would tell this story, my four-year-old son would be enthralled. It was just the most fabulous tale in the world to him. He wanted to hear it over and over. And he wanted to start planting his own tomatoes.

Living the Dream of Eve

Children aren't dumb. One of the big differences between us and them is that we've seen more of the world than they have. Often, that translates into valuable life experience, but sometimes it just means we're more jaded than they are. In the case of Moshe and his tomato plant, I am convinced that a child's unabashed wonder and joy is the more genuine human response to the saga of the tomato plant. A little child knows to pay homage to its spectacular journey from seed to stalk. A grown-up's failure to stand in awe at the tomatoes he puts in his supermarket bag is not, by comparison, anything to be proud of.

So Cain chooses to be a farmer. A strange coincidence, wouldn't you say? Eve exclaims that she has become a partner with God in creating new life. And then, Cain, her son, chooses his own path to that same thrilling goal. He is not a woman. He cannot bear fruit of the womb. But he can do the next best thing. He can cultivate the fruit of the land. He can do through land what Eve does through her body. He can place a seed in that which is fertile, cultivate the growing plant, and become a partner with the Divine in the wondrous unfolding of life.

Cain's name and his profession both point to the intoxicating wonder of the tomato plant. Eve's jubilant exclamation is the seed of Cain's name, and Cain, in turn, devotes his life to planting seeds – seeds which carry forth his mother's dream, bringing it to fruition in the new dimension of agriculture.

Our quest to understand Cain, though, is not over yet. For all of this, somehow, must be relevant to the rest of the story – to jealousy, offerings, and murder. In order for us to see how, we need to look again at Eve's exclamation of wonder, for there is something just a little bit odd about what she is saying. Instead of exclaiming, as we might have expected, that she has "created" [Hebrew: *barati*] a little man with God, or that she has "formed" [*yatzarti*] a little man with God, she says something else entirely. She says *kaniti*…that she has "acquired" a man with God.

What does she mean by such strange words? The oddity of her declaration cannot be dismissed as incidental, for it is precisely that "odd" part of what she says that is the genesis of Cain's name: Kayin is named for her word "kaniti", I have acquired.

Eve was trying to say something more. And that thought, whatever it was, found living expression in her son. Now we just have to figure out what it was.

ॐ Chapter Six
What Kind of "With"?

So Cain derives his name from his mother's declaration that she has acquired a man with God. We pointed out above that Eve's use of the word "acquire" is a bit odd. Truth to tell, though, this is not the only oddity in Eve's declaration. Something else is a bit strange as well. It has to do with the way Eve says that she has partnered "with" God.

If you were a Hebrew speaker, and you wanted to say that you had done something "with" someone else, how would you say it? Which Hebrew word would you choose for "with"? The word you would immediately, instinctively reach for would be "*im*". You can grab your dictionary and look it up. The word "im" appears everywhere in the Bible, and it is the most basic and plain way to say "with".

But this is not the word Eve uses. She uses the word "*et*". This, too, is a common word in the Bible, and "et" *can* mean "with", at least occasionally. Nine times out of ten, though, "et" means something else entirely. It performs a particular grammatical function that would be entirely out of place in Eve's sentence. We'll talk more about what "et" *usually* means shortly, but, for now, suffice it to say that Eve avoids the far more common word for "with", ("im") and uses the much more jarring, seemingly out-of-place "et" instead. Why would she do that?

From Creator to Owner

Well, first things first. Eve talks about "acquiring", rather than "creating". Is there a relationship between the two words; that is, the word we would have expected her to use ("create") and the word she actually uses ("acquire")?

Clearly, the words *are* related. "Acquiring" conjures up notions of "having" or "owning", and, indeed, a creator could be said to "have" or "own" the things he or she creates. He might be said to "acquire" them through the act of creating them. So creation, we might say, leads to ownership, right?

Well, sort of, but not necessarily. Creation *can* lead to ownership, but it doesn't have to. Let's stop and define our terms here. When I say that I own something, this means that I am asserting my right to control the thing and to keep you from using it. Now, after I make something, I *can* decide to assert this right if I want to, but I don't have to. I could alternatively decide that what I've made is open to the world, and people can use it freely. If I make a software program, I can file a patent and assert my exclusive rights over it, or I can put it up on my website and declare it "freeware". It is up to me.

The act of creation, then, sets up a choice. The choice concerns my relationship to that which I've created. Will I choose to assert my control over it? Will I choose to *own* it? Eve, at least in her own mind, seems to have made this journey from "creator" to "acquirer" – she, along with God, has "acquired" this little man. Which leads us to ask: why, exactly, would a creator choose to make this journey to ownership?

When It's Not About Money Anymore

The most obvious motivation for a creator to assert his rights of ownership, I suppose, would be economic. If I own something, I can sell or trade it for other things of value. But there are certain things which are "ours" that we don't own in an economic kind of way – children come to mind – and unless Eve was intending to put Cain up for sale on the slave market, it's doubtful that financial gain is what she has in mind when she calls Cain "hers." Indeed, the lure of cash does not by any means exhaust the list of reasons I might want to "own" that which I create. Stephen King has a lot of money already, maybe more than he can use, but he still makes sure to copyright books. Why?

A deeper reason a creator wishes to exert ownership, I think, is a sense of pride in what he's made. By this, I don't mean pride in a bad sense; I mean it in a natural sense. What I've made is an expression of who I am. It is precious to me. I poured resources, energy, and ingenuity into its making, and I want to make sure the thing maintains its integrity once it is released into the world at large.

To clarify the point: calling myself the owner of what I've made is not necessarily a selfish act. I may well be ready to part with what I've made, to bestow it as a gift to others or to the world, but I still want to make sure the world receives what I intended to give it. I don't want my precious creation to be adulterated or corrupted by other well-meaning but misguided hands. Sometimes, I assert that what I've made is mine merely in order to protect what I think is its core identity.

Speaking personally, I can certainly relate to the impulse of a creator to see himself as an owner. A number of years ago, I was asked by a local organization to develop a series of classes on the "Meaning of Life According to Judaism." It seemed like a hopelessly vague and probably fruitless assignment. But after many days and weeks of work, I had finally put together something that, well, I really liked. I was truly proud of the outcome. And all of a sudden, I felt terribly reluctant to do what I had said I would do. I was supposed to teach the course to a number of teachers, who would then go out and teach it to students. But I didn't want to do that anymore. I feared that the organization that had commissioned the project didn't really understand what I had put together, and I worried that the delicate tapestry I had constructed would become corrupted in the hands of others who didn't care about it as much as I did. I can't say I'm proud of feeling this way but, for better or worse, I just wasn't prepared to give up control over what I had made. It was too dear to me.

In using the word "acquire" rather than "create," perhaps Eve was making some sort of journey from creator to owner. Not an owner in a base, economic sense, but in a fuller, even spiritual sense. What she created with God was not something trivial or incidental, but something imbuing her life with new sanctity and meaning. Indeed, Eve's very name speaks to this life goal. Eve, or in Hebrew *Chava*, is short for *em kol chai*, "Mother of All Life." The fruits of her partnership with the Almighty are not incidental to who she is; they help *define* who she is. The child would be both hers and God's, come what may. Cain mattered to her in the deepest possible way.*

From *Im* to *Et*

But to truly understand Eve, we must confront her unusual use of "et" instead of "im." While "et" *can* be used to mean "with" (as Eve seems to use it here), that is not the usual, dominant meaning of the word. What, in fact, does "et" usually mean?

Before I answer, let me make my case as to why it's even important for us to know this. Why should we be so concerned with the *other* meaning of "et," if that's not the meaning that Eve intends?

The answer is this: when it comes to Hebrew, synonyms (like, for example, "et" and "im") are a tricky business. You always have to ask why there are two words for an idea when one would have done just fine. More often than not, the two synonymous words don't mean exactly the same thing; they are instead slightly different flavors of the same ice cream. We saw an example of this a

---

* Indeed, the very word "matter" may well derive from the Latin and Greek word for mother, "mater."

while back when we were talking about the words "eiphoh" and "ayeh" in connection with Adam and Eve. These two words, each ostensibly meaning "where," actually signify two very different questions: "where?" vs. "where have you gone?" Likewise, when it comes to "with," if there are two Hebrew words for this idea, it may well be that the idea itself comes in two different flavors.

How do you discern the taste of each flavor, the precise meaning of each term? One way to do it is to look for alternative meanings of each word. If "et" has a primary meaning and a secondary meaning, it may well be that the secondary meaning derives from the primary one. The kind of "with" that "et" expresses may be influenced by whatever else this word "et" really means.

Getting At *Et*

So now, back to our question: what does "et" usually mean, when it doesn't mean "with"? Well, I'm glad you asked. The question, though, isn't so easy to answer, for the primary meaning of the word "et" has no English counterpart. It is a grammatical utility tool unique to the Hebrew language. It provides a bridge, a link, between a verb and a direct object. In English, we don't have a need for any special words to perform this task. We just put the verb and direct object right next to each other and call it a day. In Hebrew, though, "et" would be inserted between the two to complete the link.

Here's a quick example. In English, if you struck a little round thing, you would say, "I hit the ball," and it would be clear to all what you meant. In Hebrew, though, you wouldn't say it that way. You would use the word "et" to create the link between verb and object. You would say *hikeiti "et" hakadur* – or, "I hit 'et' the ball."

So allow me to be the first to congratulate you – you are now an expert in Hebrew grammar, and there, it wasn't even so painful, was it? But the real prize is that you are now in a better position to understand the Bible. For now that you know what "et" *usually* means, you can see what it might have meant when Eve used it to mean "with."

Co-Subject or Tool?

In English, as in Hebrew, the word "with" admits of two meanings. I can say that I wrote this chapter with a co-author. (I didn't.) Or I can say I wrote it with a word-processor. (I did.) In each case, I am using the same word "with," but I mean vastly different things:

- One kind of "with" denotes full companionship; the other denotes subservience.
- One kind of "with" indicates an equal partnership; the other, an unequal partnership.
- One kind of "with" is denoted by "im"; the other by "et."

The "im" type of "with" points to a co-subject – another author, for example, who along with me, plans, plots and writes the chapter. The "et" kind of "with", though, doesn't point to another subject at all. It points to an object – a tool that I make use of to achieve my goal.

TABLE I: "IM" VS. "ET"

I, **with** Sam, my fictional friend,	*Subject Clause*	I
wrote	*Verb*	Wrote
this chapter	*Object Clause*	this chapter **with** my word processor
"Im" type of "with"		"Et" type of "with"

In a curious way, perhaps the two meanings of "et" really *are* the same. "Et," when used as a grammatical link, points to an object in a sentence. And "et," when used to mean *with*, points to an object, too. It indicates what a subject uses to get something done.

So now, one more time – when Eve said "I *acquired* a man *with* God," what was she really saying? The two halves of Eve's marvelously concise statement mesh to form a fascinating whole. Eve perceives herself a partner with the Almighty in the sacred and miraculous act of creation. The fruit of this partnership matters to her, means everything to her; she has acquired, not merely created, and the product of this creativity expresses the essence of who she is. And yet this is not a partnership of equals. One partner is subject; the other is object. One is innovator; the other, a tool.

But which partner is which? Which is the innovator, and which is the tool?

.

ℰ Chapter Seven
Thomas Edison and the Glassblower

The year is 1879. The place: Menlo Park, New Jersey. You are a glassblower. But it is merely a job, you are quite sure – not a life's calling. Orphaned at a young age, you dropped out of high school to take over your father's glassworks shop. Since then, you've reliably provided for your mother and sisters, and you are proud of that. But sometimes, late at night, you lie awake. You've never quite shaken off the urge to be a part of something larger.

During the years you've spent in your humble shop, the realms of industry and technology have exploded with innovation. The telegraph came into being just a few years ago, and the world will never be the same. Things that seemed the stuff of science fiction are becoming a reality. It is all happening in your lifetime. You would give anything to be a part of it.

Alas, though, fate and fortune have had other plans. Day after day you ply your trade, and customers come and go. But one day, something curious happens. A man comes into your shop with an unusually keen interest in the work you are doing. He looks at the delicate balls of hollow glass you've constructed and compliments you on your skill. Then he tips his hat and leaves.

Behold, the Bush Was Ablaze, But It Was Not Being Consumed…

One night, about a month later, you are walking home from work when something catches your eye. All the houses are dark, save one. At the far end of the block, a light shines from a living room window. You walk up to investigate the possible danger – perhaps a candle has been left burning unintentionally – and are startled to find that the source of the light is not a candle at all. Instead, there is a man hunched over a glowing ember, enclosed in glass. The ember is white hot, its shine is bright, but strangely, it doesn't seem to be burning…

Suddenly, the ember flares and the man recoils. The glass shatters, and the house is plunged into smoky darkness. You hurry away, but in the glare of the ember, you have caught a glimpse of the man's face. It was that fellow you met in your shop a month ago.

That night, you can't stop thinking about the strange light. A voice inside you urges that something momentous is afoot. You feel that somehow, on the sleepy streets of Menlo Park, the world is about to change forever. You throw off the covers, pull on a bathrobe, and hurry down the street to that house. The man opens the door and greets you with a smile. "I've been waiting for you," he tells you with a wink. "I could use the services of a good glassblower."

At three in the morning that cold December night, Thomas Edison tells you everything. You hear about his quest to harness electricity to create a lasting, reliable form of illumination. For the first time, he tells you, people will have the benefit of light without the aid of the sun or a flame. He shows you his sketches and his calculations. He is almost ready to unveil his invention. But he is missing just one thing. That is why, he tells you, it was so fortunate that you showed up at his house this evening.

For Edison's new "light bulb" to actually work, the ember – or the filament, as he calls it – needs to be encased in a complete vacuum. There can't be any air whatsoever in the inner chamber, or the filament will ignite and the device will explode. He needs, he tells you, the services of a good glassblower, someone who can create a hollow ball of glass filled with a perfect vacuum.

You tell him you can do it, that he's come to the right man. You've been making glass ornaments all your life, and it's not so hard to suck the air out of the sphere as you seal it. You return to his shop the next evening, and you easily encase his contraption in the clear, sealed chamber he has been looking for. Edison turns a switch and the dream he told you about takes shape before your eyes. The carbonized sewing thread inside the crystal orb begins to glow steadily and evenly. The seconds turn to minutes, and minutes to hours. The light continues to shine. You and Edison have done it.

Days later, you both invite the entire neighborhood to Edison's makeshift garage laboratory. You and he have rigged it from end to end with wires and with these new-fangled light bulbs. It's a moonless night and the sky is black, but with one flick of the switch, all that changes. The entire laboratory is illuminated with the light of a hundred tiny suns. The men and women who have come to watch erupt in spontaneous applause.

Your dream has come true before your eyes. The age of the incandescent light bulb has dawned, and you, the humble glassblower from a small New Jersey hamlet, have been a part of it. What more could you ask for?

The Danger of the Dream

The story seems a happy one. But it won't necessarily end that way. Troubled waters may lie just below the surface of this idyllic little scene. The trouble begins this way.

Your partnership with Mr. Edison may have started with a chance encounter, but it is not a trivial opportunity. Its possibilities touch the core of who you are and what you want to be.

Glassblowing is all very nice, but you don't think that's what your life is truly about. What's really made your stay on earth meaningful, you feel, is this great opportunity to create on a grand scale – this chance to seize nature boldly by the throat and make something new out of it, to harness the fearsome power of lightning in a glass ball and transform people's lives forever.

Now consider this: What happens when something you make means so much to you that you view the wondrous creation as an expression of your deepest self, that you feel a need to safeguard it assiduously; that you see yourself not merely as its "creator" but as its "acquirer," as its rightful owner? On the one hand, there is nothing evil or malevolent about making this jump from "creator" to "owner." But it produces certain challenges. Especially when that which one cherishes was not made by him alone, but was made in partnership with someone else.

Who's Who?

The first great challenge is this: Will you see this partnership for what it truly is, or will you see it as you wish it to be? Let's talk about you, the glassblower, and Mr. Edison. Who is the major partner in this endeavor, and who is the minor partner?

Well, let's see. Edison came up with the idea, sketched out the plans, did the calculations, spotted the pitfalls, planned how to correct them, and designed the first working model of the light bulb. And you were the glassblower who filled an order for a ball of glass with nothing inside.

It seems pretty clear that you are the minor partner. But that's not necessarily how you would choose to see it. It is a difficult thing to be the junior partner in your life's dream. And in any case, there *is* another way to look at things…

It's been five years since my first, fateful meeting with Edison. As I'm leaving the office one day, I glance behind me at the words emblazoned across the entry way to our new corporate headquarters, Edison & Fohrman Electric Works. And for the first time, I feel vaguely uneasy.

"How come it has to be 'Edison & Fohrman' Electric Works?" I wonder to myself. "Why sure, the sign guys had to put one of our names first, and 'E' does come before 'F,' if we follow alphabetical order – but really now, couldn't it just as easily have said 'Fohrman & Edison' Electric Works? I mean, let's face it. Thomas is a nice guy and all, and far be it from me to actually bring this up with him, but, you know he'd never be anywhere without a good glassblower like me in his life. Why, he'd still be out there in his garage with light bulbs exploding all around him. Sure, he came up with all the plans; but, it is one thing to think of things, it's another to put them into practice. You know, I really should talk to those sign guys about reversing the names..."

Eve and Cain

Eve's exclamation upon delivering the first human child may well have been her attempt to grapple with this very dilemma. How does one balance the burning passion to create new life – the sense that one's destiny and purpose is bound up in this astonishing ability to create a new person – with the reality that one is the junior partner in this enterprise?

Eve declares that she has acquired a little man with God – *kaniti ish et HaShem*. As explained in the previous chapter, the word "et" conveys the kind of "with" that normally signifies an unequal partnership, a partnership of subject and object, of actor and tool. But the precise meaning of Eve's phrase is difficult and elusive. Who, exactly, is the actor, and who is the tool?

Does she mean that God is the primary partner and she, the vehicle by which the child came to be, is secondary? This would certainly seem to reflect the reality of the situation. God is the architect of the system of reproduction; God designed it; and God alone stands behind its intricate biochemistry. Eve brings this

129

design into the world in a *practical* sense; she is the glassblower, as it were, providing a vehicle through which the Almighty's artistry can find its physical expression.

Is this what Eve means? It could be. Here is the argument in favor of translating her words that way: "Et," the "unequal" kind of "with," might mean something like "along with" – as in, "I went shopping *along with* you." Here, I am secondary to you; the sense of the phrase is that I am tagging along with you. Something like this, for example, seems to be what the Bible has in mind when it says that Joseph was shepherding "et" his brothers (Genesis 37:2). Joseph was shepherding *along with* them; he was tagging along, as it were. Similarly, Eve may mean that she has created this little man *along with* God, the primary Creator.

But it may not be so simple. As a matter of fact, even in the case of Joseph, it may not be so simple. Look again at that verse about Joseph and his brothers. This time, however, let's view the words in their larger context:

"Joseph was seventeen years old, and he was shepherding 'et' his brothers through sheep…and he brought back bad reports [about his brothers] to his father" (Genesis 37:2).

There is something incongruous in that sentence. What is it supposed to mean that Joseph was shepherding along with his brothers "through" sheep? Yes, you heard right, that *is* what the original text says. The Hebrew prefix *b*, placed here before the word "sheep," signifies either "through," "with," "concerning," or some similar preposition. None of these words easily make sense in the verse, and indeed the phrase "shepherding *through* sheep" appears nowhere else in the entire Torah.

The verse, I think, suggests a secondary level of meaning. On the one hand, yes, Joseph is shepherding *along with* his brothers, and what they are shepherding is sheep. But on another level, what Joseph is really tending is not sheep at all. He is *tending his brothers*, and he is doing it *through the medium* of sheep.

Let me explain. Think about what Joseph is really doing in this verse. He is using the opportunity of shared work-time with his brothers to bring back reports about his brothers to their father. Thus, while ostensibly shepherding *with* his brothers, he is in fact tending *them* – using sheep in order to do so. The brothers are more like the direct object of Joseph's shepherding than co-subjects along with Joseph.

When it comes to Eve, a similar kind of double meaning may reside in the verse. On the one hand, Eve declares that she has created this child *along with* God. But recall that God appears after the word "et" in a spot usually reserved for a direct object. Perhaps a secondary meaning whispers something else: God, her partner in this act, has been *the means through which* she has been able to acquire this man-child. She has used the services of God to bring about her dream.

The difference between one meaning and another is subtle, but it is not inconsequential. In fact, it may be that the discrepancy between them becomes fully recognizable only in the next generation – in the hands of the man Eve has acquired, in the hands of *Kayin*/Cain.

Indeed, how the glassblower views Edison is not just an issue of attitude and perspective. It also influences how he acts toward Edison; it influences the kind of gifts the glassblower might choose to give him. And therein, I believe, lies the key to understanding the mystery of Cain's rejected offering.

₹ Chapter Eight
The Keys to the Heavenly Cookie Jar

The story of Cain and Abel, the story of humanity's first offerings, raises a knotty theological question: Does God really need these offerings, or *any* offerings, for that matter? Is God really sated by the odor of meat rising from the altar? Is it conceivable that the Master of the Universe, the Creator of all Life, would need sacrifices of animal or plant life to keep Him happy? It seems an insult to our concept of the Creator to assume any of this.

Keep these issues in the back of your mind as we wrap up our look at the glassblower and his friend Mr. Edison.

Edison and the Glassblower, Redux

It's been almost a year since the incorporation of Edison and Fohrman Electric Works. Thomas and I are busy planning our gala, first anniversary party, to which virtually the whole town will be invited. It occurs to me that this would be a good time for me to give my partner, Thomas, a gift…

Earlier, we saw that the glassblower who assisted Edison in creating the light bulb had a fateful choice to make. Would he have the courage to see himself as he really is – as the junior partner in the venture – or would he invert that reality, fancying *himself* the primary innovator, with his friend Thomas a mere apprentice?

But it is not just a matter of how the glassblower chooses to *think* about Edison. It is also a matter of how he *acts* towards him. For when the glassblower decides that he really should give a gift to his partner, Thomas, what precisely is his motivation?

When Prudence Is Not a Virtue

One motivation the glassblower might have for his gift is pure gratitude. If the glassblower is emotionally courageous, if he can assimilate the truth about his relationship with Edison, he will recognize the overwhelming debt he owes his friend. And he will want to find a way to express that recognition to him:

> *"Through Edison, I have had a hand in one of the greatest inventions of all time; I have risen beyond my wildest hopes to become a part of history. I am eternally grateful that he has allowed me to have a small part in all this. I have to find some way to express this to him…"*

But clear-eyed gratitude is not the only motivation our glassblower might have. What if he finds it too painful to recognize he is only a junior partner in his life's dream? What if, instead of facing that truth head-on, our glassblower chooses to invert reality and adopt the fantasy that he, not Edison, is the primary partner in the venture? He could then surmise that he is not really indebted to Edison; that, if anything, Edison is indebted to *him*.

This doesn't mean our friend is going to nix the idea of giving Edison a gift. It just means that there's a different motive behind the gift. Whatever the glassblower tells himself, in the back of his mind he *knows* he needs Edison, and that at all costs, he must preserve his relationship with him:

"You know, Thomas and I are pretty chummy right now – but you never can be too careful. What if some other glassblower tries to crash this party and weasel his way into Edison's confidence? I mean, I know Thomas would be a fool to drop me for someone else, but Thomas has always been a bit naïve about the intricacies of glassblowing. It might just be prudent for me to buy him a little something in advance of next week's party..."

This second kind of gift is very different than the first. It is not really about gratitude; it is about insurance. It is not an expression of personal feelings so much as it is a concession to business necessities. There are costs to doing business, and one of those costs is keeping the people that you need happy.

These differences in motivation begin in the mental realm, in the private realm of the giver's mind. But these differences don't stay private for long. They invariably express themselves in the nature of the gift one chooses to give.

A person expressing a profound sense of gratitude gives the best he can. A person buying an insurance policy is looking for a reasonable deal.

If the Almighty Has No Needs, How Can I Give Him Anything?

Let's return to the question we raised at the beginning of this chapter. Does God really need what we are trying to give Him? The answer must be that an offering, in its genuine religious sense, is not an attempt to fulfill the "needs" of God. The Almighty doesn't *have* any needs – that, indeed, is why they call Him "all-mighty." The unexamined false premise that gave rise to our question was the notion that gifts are always meant to fulfill needs. That is not always true. Among the other reasons we give gifts is something we call "gratitude."

Gratitude has very little to do with a recipient's needs. Because this is so, it is not crucial that gifts of gratitude be expensive or abundant. But it *is* important that one give his best. The gift might be as simple as a single rose picked from your garden, but it will be the *best* of those roses. Anything less fails to say what you want it to say.

Recently, a student of mine phoned to discuss a gift that the class was planning to give me. Usually such end-of-year gifts are meant to be surprises, but this student broke the rules and figured that he, on behalf of the class, would just ask me what I wanted. He made an interesting stipulation, though. My laptop had been stolen the week before, and he remarked, "Frankly, we could just buy you another laptop, but we know you'll get that for yourself one way or the other. We want to give you something special, so how about a gift certificate for a gourmet dinner and tickets to a terrific new play for you and your wife?"

When a gift is meant to express gratitude, it's not really about fulfilling the needs of the recipient. The thing I needed most was a new laptop. But, unlucky for me, that was beside the point. The gift needed to be special, and a laptop was simply too pedestrian to qualify. Strangely, but perhaps appropriately, the "specialness" of the gift – at least in the mind of this student – seems to have had an inverse relationship to how much I needed it. Instead, "only the finest" – the gourmet meal and tickets to the play – would do.

Expressions of gratitude such as these can help build relationships. Ironically, though, not all gifts are so constructive. When a gift masquerades as gratitude but is really a glorified insurance policy, it doesn't help our relationship with the recipient one little bit.

God and the Heavenly Cookie Jar

Earlier, in chapter five, we saw that Cain derives his name, Kayin, from Eve's declaration of awe at his birth. We also saw that Cain, through farming, actualizes his name. He, like his mother before him, devotes himself to the thrilling creation of new life – in his case, seedlings – in partnership with God. Yet Cain, in offering a gift to his Divine partner, chooses to give something that is merely average. Why would he do that? Is Cain giving a free-flowing gift of unmitigated gratitude, or is he giving a calculated bargaining chip? Is it about "what can I give," or "how much can I afford?"

Remember, there was a potentially dark side to Eve's declaration. She was not just "creator" but "acquirer," and in her exalted partnership with God, it was not entirely clear who was the vehicle for whose creativity. Eve's difficulty is perhaps compounded in the next generation by her son Cain. If Eve's challenge was to *think* with integrity, to maintain cognizance of her role as junior partner with the Divine, maybe her son's challenge was to *act* with integrity – to relate to the Almighty from a position of gratitude, not bribery. And perhaps it was here that he failed.

Beyond Logic

If this was the root of Cain's failure, his behavior was certainly understandable, even logical. Bargaining chips are more rational than free-flowing gratitude. After all, God is very powerful. He holds the keys to the Great Heavenly Cookie Jar, and we all want what's in that jar. But if we are not careful, the need to get those things can loom larger and larger until this need crowds everything else out.

Ultimately, when the gift you give is little more than a spiritual insurance policy to make sure you get what you want from God, you may, ironically, be creating distance with that gift, not closeness. The nature of this distance is something we have yet to explore, but for now, suffice it to say that when a recipient refuses such a gift, what he is really saying is, "Try again – you're not in the insurance business. This isn't what our relationship is meant to be about."

And that, in effect, is what God is telling Cain by rejecting his offering. But the Almighty does not *just* reject Cain's offering. God also provides Cain some words of guidance to accompany that rejection. The meaning of this guidance, though, is maddeningly elusive. Deciphering God's words to Cain is therefore the next task that lies before us.

ใ Chapter Nine
Cain and the Kitten

Just before Cain goes for that fateful stroll in the fields with his brother, the Almighty speaks to him. This is what God says:

> "Why are you angry and why has your face fallen? Is it not the case that if you do well, then lift up! And if you don't do well, then sin lies crouching at the door, its desire is unto you, and you can rule over it." (Genesis 4:6–7)

What do these cryptic words mean? And, whatever they mean, why is it that Cain needs to hear them right now?

Beyond Brownie Points

A cursory glance at the words might lead you to believe that God's speech is a standard-issue religious exhortation to be a better person, something along the lines of: "You'd better be nice! If you are, God will reward you. But if you're mean, He'll punish you." Yet it seems that something more complex is going on. For while God *does* talk about two alternatives that lie before Cain – a fork in the road where he can choose either good or its opposite – still, what

God says next is enigmatic and has little in common with conventional "brownie points vs. fire-and-brimstone" style thinking.

First, the Lord never suggests to Cain that he will be rewarded for good conduct. The text says something else entirely, that if Cain "does well," then, "*lift up!*" Now what precisely this means is a very good question – we'll get back to it – but it doesn't sound as if God is promising Cain a tangible reward for doing the right thing. Something else is going on.

And let's proceed a bit further. What exactly will happen to Cain if he chooses the other path, if he doesn't "do well"? You might have expected God to speak about punishments here – if not full-fledged warnings of fire and brimstone, then at least some sort of repercussion to discourage bad behavior. Instead, though, God says something tantalizing, but a bit confusing: "*If you do not do well, sin lies crouching at the door.*"

Now, what exactly does *that* mean? Whatever it means, it doesn't sound like God is imposing a punishment. If anything, it sounds like God is saying that Cain, by choosing evil, will somehow become vulnerable to sin. Sin will be like a crouching beast ready to pounce and overcome him. But that idea is itself puzzling. For if Cain chooses evil – well, *that itself* is a sin, isn't it? So why say vulnerability to sin is a consequence? The verse seems to have it backwards, no?

Talking Cain Off the Bridge

So we have some difficulties in understanding God's words here, and we'll get back to these issues; but, in the meantime, let's not lose sight of the forest for the trees. Bottom line, what seems to be the overall message of the speech? What is the general tone of the Almighty's words? What is God "more or less" saying?

Well, given the placement of this speech – it occurs one sentence before Cain murders his brother – it seems logical that the Lord may have been trying to talk Cain off the bridge, as it were. The Almighty was surely aware of the violence of which Cain was capable. Perhaps the speech was a last attempt to rouse Cain into

seeing an alternative course of action beside the dark path lying ominously before him.

But if the speech is an attempt to talk Cain off the bridge, God's tactics seem puzzling. The verse tells us that Cain was angry and he was crestfallen. Well, if someone you knew were angry and crestfallen and you were trying to get them to reconsider some kind of disastrous, irreversible step they were about to take, how would you go about it? What kind of tone would you adopt?

Speaking for myself, I would probably try to sound empathetic and reassuring. "It's okay; I understand how you feel; it must be hard" – something along those lines. But that is hardly the tone of God's speech. Instead, God forcefully challenges Cain. As a matter of fact, He goes as far as to question Cain's right to feel the way he does: "Why are you angry and why has your face fallen?"

When I was growing up, I was often told, "You can't help how you *feel*, but you *can* help what you do about it." If you feel angry, fine; but you don't have to act on that anger. In the words of His speech, though, the Almighty seems to take issue with that advice. Apparently, Cain *can* help how he feels about it. Cain is crestfallen, and he is angry – but he shouldn't be. His perspective needs to change.

Why is it so vital that Cain abandon his current set of feelings? Because, I think, those feelings indicate something. They indicate that Cain has misinterpreted what has gone on between himself and God. And only by correcting his view of the situation will Cain be able to steer himself away from a course that leads straight to murder.

How Do You Change Your Feelings?

Anger and depression make good bed-fellows; they often go together. Each is basically a passive emotional response. Anger and depression both take for granted that the source of our woes is located outside ourselves, that we have been betrayed by others, or have been victimized by forces beyond our control. And while this may sometimes be the case, it can also be an exaggeration. More

often than not, we *do* have choices available to us, even if we are not always prepared to recognize them. Once we see the choices, our anger and depression begin to evaporate.

Harriett Lerner's book, *The Dance of Anger**, paints a scenario that nicely illustrates the point. It goes more or less like this. Imagine you and your roommate have a pet. For our purposes, let's say it's a kitten.One night the kitten wakes you with some strange meowing. It is two-thirty in the morning, and you are concerned. You turn to your roommate, and a conversation ensues between the two of you that goes roughly like this:

> YOU: "She really doesn't sound right. I think we should call the vet."
> ROOMMATE: "What do you mean, call the vet? It's the middle of the night!
> YOU: "I don't know. She really sounds pretty bad. I think we should call the vet…"
> ROOMMATE: "Look, just go back to sleep. She probably swallowed a hairball."
> YOU: "Are you sure we shouldn't just call the vet?"
> ROOMMATE: "Good night!"

You both go back to sleep, and when you wake up in the morning, the kitten is dead.

Now take a deep breath and ask yourself: how are you going to feel toward your roommate when morning comes and you discover the lifeless kitten lying next to your bed? You are likely to be enraged: "It's all your fault! Here I was, telling you that we should take the kitten to the vet, and all you could think about was getting a good night's sleep! And now the kitten is dead."

Whether you like it or not, though, the reality is otherwise. You were not the victim of circumstances beyond your control.

---

* Harriet Lerner, *The Dance of Anger: A Woman's Guide to Changing the Patterns of Intimate Relationships* (Harper, 1997), 125–126.

You were not betrayed by your sleep-seeking roommate. You had free will. There were choices open to you, choices you refused to grab hold of. No one forced you to get permission from your roommate before calling the vet. You could have called had you wanted to. If you feel angry or depressed here, it is because you choose to see yourself as helpless, a victim of your lousy, insensitive roommate. But in fact, you weren't a victim at all.

Feeling angry, Cain locates the source of his problem outside of himself, in God. No one can control God, and as long as that's the problem, you're nothing but a victim. But that wasn't the reality. The core of his problem lay entirely in the choices Cain himself was making, in the nature of the relationship he was building with God, and this was a realm entirely *within* his control. The first step off the bridge, then, is letting go of anger and depression and reclaiming this element of control.

The Perils of Neutrality

So all in all, Cain is being given an antidote to his feelings of anger and depression. You have choices, God says, the ball is in your court. "If you do well, then, lift up!" What had been downcast before – Cain's face ("Why has your face fallen...") – can now be raised. Cain will be able to look himself in the eye, as it were, when he stares at the mirror in the morning. When we seize our power to act in a positive way, we begin to lift up our faces again in the ultimate gesture of self-respect.

Of course, when choices are available, there is always the option of choosing poorly, too: "And if you don't do well, then sin lies crouching at the door..." Earlier, we got stuck on this phrase. How could the consequence of sin be vulnerability to sin? But when the verse talks about "not doing well," who says that's the same as committing a sin? After all, the text doesn't say: "If you do evil," then sin lies crouching at the door; instead, it says "*if you do not do well.*" Not doing good isn't the same thing as doing evil. It is simply being neutral. Maybe God is saying something like the following:

Why has your face fallen? If you are active, if you seek out the good – you can lift up your face. And if you are neutral – if you do not act positively – you can't tread water. While being neutral is not itself an evil, it does leave you vulnerable to evil. Sin lies crouching at the door, and even the most well-intentioned neutral party can still become its prey.

An interesting speech, we might conclude. And let's even grant for the moment that we are right in interpreting it this way. We still have yet to address a nagging question: why does Cain need to hear this right now? It's all very nice, these words about neutrality and activism, about vulnerability to sin. It sure seems like an inspiring thing to put in the Bible somewhere, maybe tucked comfortably into a suitable corner of Deuteronomy. But what is it doing right here, right now? Beyond the general idea that Cain can act if he chooses to, how are these words about neutrality and vulnerability uniquely relevant to Cain and to the situation in which he finds himself?

Back to Eden

In the coming pages, we'll explore that issue and begin to put into place the final pieces of our look at this story. But first, let me leave you with a little tip.

We discussed earlier the striking montage of connections existing between the Cain and Abel story and the story of humanity's expulsion from Eden. Both Adam and Cain hear the Divine question, "Ayeh?" Both Adam and Cain express fear and hide from God. Both Adam and Cain suffer exile. And both Adam and Cain are condemned to experience difficulty farming. But the truth is that the connections between the Cain story and the aftermath of the Tree of Knowledge do not end even there. There remains one final parallel hidden within the text of the speech we have just studied. If you look carefully at that speech, you'll realize that an entire section of it is lifted virtually verbatim from words that God had once told someone else, not thirty verses earlier.

144

Of all the Eden connections we have seen thus far, this one is the most shocking and disturbing, at least when you first see it. If you find the parallel, you'll know exactly what I'm talking about. Yet it is in the mystery of this last Eden connection that we will finally learn the full import of what God told Cain in the moments before Abel's murder.

𝒞 Chapter Ten

Can Desire Be Divorced from Need?

I have a favor to ask of you. It is an unusual request, but I have my reasons, trust me. The request is this:

> *If you happen to be flipping through this book and have opened randomly to this chapter, you need to promise me that you'll read the whole thing, all the way to the end. If you can't make that commitment, I am going to ask you to stop right here.*

I make this unusual request because what I am about to discuss is both theologically explosive and easily misunderstood. It concerns the Bible's view of masculinity and femininity and the relationship between them. There are many who view the Bible as a tome written by men seeking to safeguard their patriarchal power, while keeping the women in their lives subjugated and docile. I myself do not share this view. But if someone with that agenda wanted to find grist for the mill, he would need look no further than the two verses to which I am about to direct your attention.

It is easy to overlook just how astonishing these two verses are. Each verse on its own seems fairly innocuous. But when you put them together, they are positively combustible. In reality, I think the verses provide only an excuse, not real evidence, for the charge that the Bible denigrates women. But that's why I need you to keep reading past the middle of this chapter. If you are going to let me show you the explosive part, you owe it to me and to yourself, to think carefully about what the words really mean. When I've had my say, take some time to think about it, and then you can make up your own mind.

Okay, so we have a deal? If you're with me this far, I'll assume that we do.

A Fearsome Analogy

I warned earlier that there was one final parallel to the world of Eden tucked away in the Cain story. It appears within God's speech to Cain. Part of this speech has been said before, back in Eden, not thirty verses earlier. Can you find what I am talking about? Listen again to the words of God's speech to Cain. As you do, ask yourself: "Where have I heard these words before?"

> Why are you angry and why has your face fallen? Is it not the case that if you do well, then lift up! And if you don't do well, then sin lies crouching at the door, its desire is unto you, yet you can rule over it.

The telltale words are the very last ones:

"...its desire is unto you, yet you can rule over it."

This concluding phrase is lifted almost verbatim from something God said earlier, just after the man and his wife ate from the Tree of Knowledge. The original words are troubling enough on their own. But when you take into account their reappearance in the Cain story, they become downright fearsome.

The first time these words appear, God is speaking to Eve.

148

After telling her that she will experience pain in childbirth, He concludes by saying to her:

> *"...your desire will be to your husband, yet he can rule over you."* (Genesis 3:16)

Do you hear the resemblance? God says to Eve that her desire will be to her husband, yet he can rule over her. That's bad enough for us modern types. But then God says to Cain, thirty verses later, that the Evil Inclination's desire is to Cain, yet Cain can rule over it.

Well, that just takes the cake, doesn't it? I mean the Bible seems to be suggesting some sort of analogy here. And it's a profoundly disturbing analogy at that. Those of you who took the SATS to get into college are no doubt familiar with these kinds of analogies. If you add it up, it sounds like Cain is analogous to Adam, and Eve is analogous to – make sure you are sitting down for this – Cain's Evil Inclination.

It seems too horrible to believe.

When It's Too Good to Be True...

An old adage says that when something seems too good to be true, it usually is. In this case, I think the converse is also true – when something seems too horrible to believe, it sometimes is exactly that – not to be believed.

In this vein, I think some healthy skepticism is in order. Is it really conceivable that the Bible considers Eve – womankind – tantamount to "sin," the anthropomorphic title given by the verse to Cain's Evil Inclination? Is the Torah viewing femininity as some evil force threatening to overtake the masculine, something men must keep at bay lest it devour them? Again, it seems too horrible to believe. But what, then, *is* the Torah trying to say to us with its not-so-subtle link between one phrase and the other?

Okay, just in case you were wondering, this is the part where you're not supposed to stop reading. The fact is that we've committed a logical error in interpreting the analogy. In general, analogies are notoriously easy to misinterpret – that, after all, is why they put them on the SATs – and this analogy is no exception. Let's step back, take a deep breath, and try again.

What if I told you that whales desperately need plankton and that cars desperately need gasoline? Both these statements are true, and we might say that an analogy exists between them. But – bear with me here – it does not follow from this that whales are basically the same as cars or that plankton is pretty much identical to gasoline. Marine biologists would surely be offended by that conclusion. Rather, what follows is that the *relationship* between whales and plankton is similar to the *relationship* between cars and gasoline. In each case, the latter provides the fuel that makes the former go.

And so it is with our analogy. Although both verses use similar language, it does not follow that Cain is like Adam, nor does it follow that Eve is like Cain's Evil Inclination. Rather, what follows is that the *relationship* between Adam and Eve – or, more broadly, between man and woman – is analogous on some level to the *relationship* that Cain is asked to develop with his Evil Inclination. And while this might not seem much better than the previous alternative, hang in there. We're just beginning to uncover what's going on.

The Four Primal Desires

Over a thousand years ago, the Rabbis of the Midrash noticed the analogy we have been wrestling with, and they had something quite intriguing to say about it. They observed that the Bible uses the Hebrew term *teshukah* (desire) in both verses we have been discussing. In tracing the various scriptural occurrences of this word, the Sages recognized a pattern. Here is what they had to say:

"There are four [basic] teshukot in the world. The teshukah of Eve for Adam, the teshukah of the Evil Inclination for

Cain, the teshukah of rain for land, and the teshukah of the Master of the Universe for humanity." (Midrash Rabbah on Genesis, 20:7)

The Sages cite additional verses (which I have not reproduced here) to substantiate each one of these conclusions, but let's focus on just these four statements. What are the Rabbis really saying?

It seems to me that they are defining the word "teshukah" – and making a sweeping, almost radical, statement in the process. Look carefully at the four examples they give: the desire of Eve for Adam, of the Evil Inclination for Cain, of rain for land, and of God for humanity – and see if you can isolate a common denominator among them.

While you are mulling that over, you might notice that some of the desires indicated by the Rabbis don't sound much like desires at all. Let's look, for example, at the last two: the desire of rain for land and the desire of the Almighty for humanity. If you were given the words "rain" and "land," and someone asked you, "Which of these two 'desires' the other," what would you say?

I would say "land" is the one with the desire. Land needs rain to nourish its crops; rain doesn't need land at all. And the same holds for "God" and "humanity." A basic tenet of theology states that God is a perfect Being who has no needs at all. So, if we are contemplating God and humans, if anything, it should be humanity that desires God. Why do the Sages have it the other way around?

When Desire is Divorced from Need

I would argue that the Sages define teshukah as something entirely different from what we usually think of when we use the word "desire." When you and I normally talk about desire, we associate desire with "need." Think about the synonyms we use for desire. When we desire a new car, we say, "I need a new car," or "I want a new car." Both "need" and "want" are connected to the idea of "lack." When I am wanting or needful, I am missing something;

when I get it, that hole in my life is filled, and my want or need is satisfied. Usually when we talk about desire, we are really talking about getting needs fulfilled.

The question you should contemplate is this: Is that the *only* kind of desire there is in this world? Or, perhaps, is "desire" a larger concept than this? Is there a desire that is not based on a sense of need, that doesn't come from some kind of lack that I have? If all my needs and wants were taken care of, would that be it? Or could I still have some sense of desire?

I think the Sages are answering that question with a resounding, "Yes!" Yes, it *is* possible to desire something even when you don't need anything. Rain doesn't need land a whit, but somehow it still "desires" land. God doesn't need people a whit either, but somehow, He still desires them. The Sages are arguing, I think, that teshukah is a code name for this special kind of desire. And it is this very kind of desire, this teshukah, that the feminine has for the masculine. And that the Evil Inclination, whatever that is, has for Cain.

So what, exactly, is the essential nature of teshukah? How are we to understand a desire that is divorced from need? And how does this shed light on the two primal teshukahs under discussion – the "desire" of the feminine for the masculine, and the "desire" of the Evil Inclination for Cain?

That's exactly what we'll look at in just a moment. But first, a little background...

₹ Chapter Eleven
The Case of the Laughing Rabbi

Why did God create the world?

It's not just an idle, philosophical question. From a religious standpoint, this innocent, child-like query packs a big theological wallop. For if God is a perfect Being, a Being who has no needs, then why would God bother creating a universe? What could a universe possibly give to a Being who doesn't need anything at all?

In the beginning of the eighteenth century, a thinker by the name of Rabbi Moshe Hayyim Luzzatto proposed what has become a classic answer to this dilemma. His answer is deceptively simple. Luzzatto said that God created the world in order to be capable of love.

The words seem clichéd, sort of like the "God is Love" bumper sticker you might see plastered to the back of someone's rusting Volkswagon Beetle. But Luzzatto lived long before the age of the Beetle, and he meant what he said seriously, not as a cliché. His argument goes as follows:

One of the axioms that most religions, Judaism included, accept about God is that God is good. But those are just words. What does it actually *mean* to be good? One of the things it means, Luzzatto says, is that one acts to benefit others. If there is no world, though, then there *are* no others that God can benefit; He exists alone in numinous solitude. God acted to create a world so that there would be other beings existing besides Himself, beings upon whom He could bestow goodness.

In short, God created the world because goodness demanded it.

The Laughing Rabbi

Now, for many years I didn't have the foggiest idea what Luzzatto was talking about. I had problems with it. Let's leave aside the question of suffering for a moment (why, in a world created out of love, there is so much hurt and pain); let's assume that there are answers to that question out there somewhere. I was troubled by an even more fundamental difficulty. How had Luzzatto solved anything? If God is not supposed to have any needs, then He shouldn't have a need to do good, to bestow kindness, either. If God has this need, it puts us right back where we started from: How could a perfect Being have needs? How could He be missing something?

I vividly remember making this point once to the dean of the yeshiva where I studied. The dean's name was Rabbi Yaakov Weinberg, may he rest in peace, and I was sitting on a couch in his office arguing my case as forcefully as I could. I gave this example to illustrate my point. Let's say a woman saves her child from death by throwing herself in front of an oncoming car to shield him. She walks away with injuries, but none as profound as the hurt she would have felt had she allowed her child to die. So, in the final analysis, she acted out of need, didn't she?

I was arguing, really, that there was no such thing as pure altruism – acting solely for the benefit of others. Every altruistic act expresses a need within the person doing it; therefore, it is the doer, not just the receiver, who benefits from it.

When I finished making my point, I awaited Rabbi Weinberg's response. As best as I can remember the conversation, he didn't answer me. Instead, he just sat across from me, and then he started laughing. When my attempts to get him to elaborate failed, he finally spoke. One day, he said, I would understand, and then, with a good natured nod, he beckoned me to the door. Our meeting was over.

Solving the Case of the Laughing Rabbi

It has taken me a while to understand the meaning of Rabbi Weinberg's laughter, but I think I finally see what he was getting at. He was alluding to the point I left you to ponder at the end of the last chapter, where I suggested that the Sages of the Midrash saw teshukah as a *desire not based upon need*. This idea seems like an oxymoron: surely *all* desires stem from my not having something I want. Yet there really *are* radically different desires out there in the world, desires that come from no sense of lack whatsoever. Where do they come from, and what makes them tick?

Ironically enough, they come from the very opposite of "need." They come from a sense of fullness. To give an analogy, they express not the desire of the half empty glass to be full, but the desire of a full glass to overflow.

Desires based on fullness are every bit as real as those based on need. In fact, one might argue, they are felt even more intensely than those based on need. Consider the following statement made by the Rabbis of the Talmud: "More than the calf wants to suckle, the mother wants to nurse" (Babylonian Talmud, *Pesachim* 112a).

Both the calf and the mother have desires. The calf is missing something; it needs nutrition from its mother. The mother, on the other hand, needs nothing. Nevertheless, it is her desire that is the stronger one. Desires based upon fullness dwarf in passion and intensity mere need-based desires.

The Nature of Love; the Essence of Teaching

To better grasp the notion of a "fullness-based" desire, let's look at an example or two.

To begin with, what do we mean when we talk about love? Different people mean different things. Some men who say, "I love her" really mean "She fulfills my needs rather nicely." She laughs at my jokes, cooks great meals, and makes me feel comfortable. But love is not just about being fed and feeling understood. On a higher plane, love is not just about what I need, but what I can give. Love means not just that I'm happy you serve my needs, but that I appreciate who you are in and of yourself, independent of what I get from you. When I love in that way, my love comes not from lack but from fullness. My affection for you doesn't come solely from your ability to fill the holes in my personality, but from the desire of a mature human being to give what he can to someone he admires and values.

A second example of this kind of desire is the impulse to teach. The Sages of the Talmud have nasty things to say about people who study their whole lives but never teach others. Why? I'll give you a theory. The Hebrew verb "to teach" (le'lamed) is identical to the verb "to study" (lilmod), except that the former, "to teach," is the intensive form of the verb (what's known as its *piel* conjugation).* When you stop to think about it, this says something profound about what it means to teach. Teaching is nothing but "studying intensively." When someone is so passionate about what he is studying that he can't help but overflow and share his learning with others – well, that's teaching.

Since teaching is just a further point on a continuum that begins with studying, it follows that when one studies and studies,

---

* Piel verbs are the same as their regular counterparts, just more intense versions of them. For example: *Lishbor* means "to break"; *le'shaber*, the *piel* form, means "to smash."

but never teaches, something is broken inside. Study that never flowers into teaching is, somehow, not the real thing.

Male and Female Desire

There are four primal teshukahs in the world, say the Sages. There are four beings full of life-force, seeking to overflow and share that gift of life with others. One of those beings is God. It should come as no surprise that a perfect Being would experience rather intensely the desire we call teshukah. The Almighty loves, not because He is needy but because He is full. He wants to share that fullness with others. And to that end, He created a world.

Another "being" possessed of life-force is rain. The land is parched without rain, the land *needs* rain – but it is rain that experiences teshukah for land. Rain wants to give land what it can. Rain becomes meaningful because of its ability to nourish and to share itself with land. Without land, rain is frustrated, restless. The desire of rain to give life to land is intense.

Another great teshukah in the world, say the Sages, is the desire of the feminine for the masculine. What is the nature of this desire?

To be sure, both men and women desire one another, but they do so for different reasons. Let's talk about men. In traditional Jewish marriage, a man gives a ring to a woman, not the other way around. The reason is that a biblical verse (Deuteronomy 22:13) describes the man as the active partner, who "takes" a woman as his wife. Now this might strike some as sexist, but I don't think the ancient Sages meant it that way. Long ago, the Sages of the Talmud wondered about this verse in Deuteronomy. Why, they asked, does the Torah state "when a man shall take a woman..." Why is he, not she, cast as the active partner in marriage and courtship?

Here is their answer: "It is comparable to a person who lost something. Who goes searching after whom? I would say: 'The person who lost something searches after that which they lost'" (Babylonian Talmud, *Kiddushin* 3b).

The Sages are alluding to something in this cryptic statement. Remember, the verse in Deuteronomy talks about a man "taking" a woman. If you search Genesis for some of the very first occurrences of the word "take" in the Bible, you will come across the following verse:

> And [the Lord] *took* one of Adam's ribs, closed up his skin, and built [the rib] he had *taken* from man into woman... (Genesis 2:20–21)

When a man "takes" a woman in marriage, what he is really doing is taking back his lost rib. The person experiencing a loss is the one who searches for what was lost. The masculine desires the feminine because a man understands, on some basic level, that he is missing his lost feminine side, and he is seeking to reunite with her.

The feminine desires the masculine for other reasons. The feminine does not have, imprinted on her soul, the sense that she is missing something without a man. Since woman was created as a whole being, she does not experience that same, masculine sense of lack within herself. Instead, the feminine desires the masculine out of teshukah. The feminine – like rain and like God – embodies a mysterious life force, and she seeks to give that gift to the masculine.

The Talmud takes for granted that, generally speaking, women want to get married more than men do (Babylonian Talmud, *Ketubbot* 75a). This assumption should not surprise us. Desires based upon fullness are always more intense than desires based merely upon lack.

"Its Desire Is unto You..."

We are now, I think, in a position to understand what God was saying to Cain in the moments before he murdered Abel. He was talking to Cain about his Evil Inclination, and he was telling him something both startling and profound: "There is a fourth primal

158

teshukah in the world. It is the teshukah, Cain, that your Evil Inclination has for you."

What God was telling Cain forces us to redefine our notion of the Evil Inclination. When we think of the Evil Inclination, we tend to think of something, well, evil. We imagine some sort of devil bent on getting us to stray, or a dark part of our soul trying to corrupt us. But that's not how God portrays it here. Is it possible that the Evil Inclination, like the Almighty Himself, like rain, like femininity, has a powerful life force to share? That it is a neutral, even benevolent force? It seems paradoxical. Why, then, would we call it "evil"?

In the coming pages we will examine more carefully this notion of the Evil Inclination, and the relationship that God warns Cain to build with it. In so doing, I think we will finally understand why the story of Cain is so intimately related to the Tree of Knowledge, and why the unique challenges facing Cain are nothing more than its misbegotten fruits.

ℰ Chapter Twelve
Cain, Creativity and the Spice of Life

E ve hears words whose echo will later speak to her son, Cain: "Your teshukah shall be to your husband, yet he can rule over you…" (Genesis 3:16). The end of the sentence sounds harsh, and one wonders whether over the centuries it was used by authoritarian husbands to justify the use of an iron hand at home. But even if the verse may have been used that way, that doesn't mean this is what it really means. In Hebrew, the verb "rule over" – *moshel* – is spelled identically to the noun *mashal*, a word that means "parable." The similarity suggests a relationship between "moshel" and "mashal," between "ruling over something" and "parables." What might this be?

Why Parables Rule

Why do people tell parables? Parables aren't just stories. They are stories meant to interpret reality. Something happens, and it seems inexplicable. When I try to make sense of what occurred, I may tell a story, a parable, which I present as comparable in some important way to what happened.

In that sense, parables "rule" over experience. An experience in and of itself is blind and raw. It comprises an almost infinite array of tiny events and subtleties and can be viewed in a myriad of ways. A good parable helps us sort out what is essential from what is incidental. A parable takes a series of events and directs our understanding of them in a particular way.

What does a good "ruler" do? He takes the raw energy of the nation he is privileged to lead and directs it toward certain ends. The energy of a nation is a blind force; it can be used in an infinite variety of ways. In submitting a budget proposal to Congress, a president is in fact setting an agenda. He is submitting his vision of where the country ought to be going together with his intention to direct the energy of the nation – its wealth – toward specific and, one hopes, productive ends. A ruler takes raw energy and decides how to make wise use of it.

If it is the teshukah, the desire, of the feminine to establish a relationship with the masculine and share her life-force with him, the masculine must responsibly decide what he will do with this gift. Newly empowered by his union with woman, man finds himself wondering what he will do with his life, how he will direct this powerful energy outside the immediate confines of their personal relationship. He must decide on goals that productively utilize what has been entrusted to him.

Looking Past the Devil in the Bright Red Suit

The echo of these ideas – of teshukah and moshel, of life-force and its direction – re-appears in Genesis, shortly after this discussion of Adam and Eve, when God speaks to Cain about his Evil Inclination: "Its teshukah will be for you, yet you can rule over it..."

We are used to thinking of the Evil Inclination as, well, evil. That is certainly understandable considering its name. But the Sages of the Midrash had other ideas. They included the Evil Inclination among the four primal forces that experience "teshukah," a desire born not of lack but of fullness. They appear to have envisioned the Evil Inclination as a life force that overflows and then seeks to share itself.

In Part One, we discussed how the Evil Inclination is often conceived as something vaguely metaphysical or blatantly childish. We might picture a devil dressed up in a bright red suit, complete with horns and tail, or an angel with a little too much time on his hands who sits above our left shoulder and whispers bad advice in our ears. But in real life, what is this thing we call the Evil Inclination?

Again, the Midrash offers a clue. According to the Bible, when the Almighty looked back on the whole of creation, He declared, "Behold, it was very good." The Rabbis of the Midrash saw this as a pronouncement about the goodness of the *entirety* of creation, even its apparently unsavory parts: "'… and behold, it was very good'; this refers to the Evil Inclination." The comment is astounding, but the Rabbis immediately clarify what they mean by raising the obvious objection:

> Can the Evil Inclination really be classified as "very good"? It seems impossible! Yet, were it not for the Evil Inclination, a man would not build a house and would not marry a woman; he would not have children and would not engage in business… (Midrash Rabbah on Genesis, 9:7)

The Evil Inclination, in real life, is neither more nor less than our passions, the desires that fuel us and make us go. These desires, far from being inherently evil, are an essential part of our humanity. A man without passion builds no house and never marries. Cut off from ambition, he in the end builds nothing worthwhile out of his life.

Of Cars and Steering Wheels

So if the Evil Inclination is so good, why is it so bad? That, I think, is precisely what God was trying to explain to Cain: "Its teshukah is to you, yet you can rule over it." Passions are not evil in and of themselves. They constitute a powerful, inherently benign life force, whose only desire, as it were, is to establish a relationship with you. They want to overflow, to give of themselves to you. But the power of these passions is awesome, and awesome power left raw and undirected can indeed lead to great evil.

If Cain "does well," if he directs his passions properly, then "lift up!" – he can lift up his face and look at himself in the mirror in the morning. But if he does not do well – if he fails to direct these passions, if he stays neutral and lets them run wild in his soul – well, that itself may not be a sin, but *sin lies crouching at the door.* It's only a matter of time before the engine we call passion, cut off from the steering wheel meant to guide it, drives its rider over the nearest cliff.

The responsibility thus devolves upon Cain to "rule" his passions: not to crush them, but to direct their power and energy as a ruler directs the energy of the nation he governs. A car isn't a car if you destroy the engine. But it's only a safe vehicle if you decide to use the steering wheel.

Why Now?

Why did God make this speech right here, right now? A talk about passion, steering wheels, and the dangers of neutrality is all very fine, but what does it have to do with what Cain is struggling with right now? I think we can assume that when the Almighty spoke the words He did to Cain, He was not just looking for an opportunity to make a good speech. Rather, He was talking directly and personally to Cain. Cain is stung by God's rejection of his offering and is contemplating harm against his brother. What guidance is this speech offering him? It is time to return to the mysterious linkage the Bible creates between this story, the episode of Cain and Abel, and the saga of Adam and Eve in the Garden of Eden.

We have discussed how the language describing the expulsion from Eden is vividly recreated in the verses detailing the aftermath of Abel's murder. God asks both Adam and Cain the very same "ayeh" question; Adam hides from God, and so does Cain; Adam suffers exile and difficulty in farming, and so does Cain. These ideas are not merely repeated from story to story; they intensify from story to story as well. With Adam, God quests after a temporarily missing person (Adam); with Cain, He quests after a permanently missing one (Abel). Adam hides momentarily; Cain forever. Adam is exiled, but can find a new home elsewhere; Cain is condemned never to call anywhere home.

The pattern of similarity and intensification suggests a basic commonality in the stories. It suggests that the story of Cain and Abel is a farther rung on a ladder that begins with the Tree of Knowledge, that the challenges befalling Cain are precisely those we might expect in a world where humanity has just partaken from the Tree of Knowledge. But why is this so? What does a tale about eating some nice-looking Forbidden Fruit have to do with a bout of sibling rivalry that unfortunately ends in murder?

The answer, in a word, is passion. Passion, and its proper role in the human psyche, are the conceptual core of both these stories. To see how this is so will require a short journey back into territory we covered in Part One. Let's refresh our memories.

Who's Afraid of the Big, Bad Snake?

Back in the Garden of Eden, the serpent's temptation exposed this question: how is humanity meant to relate to the voice of desire, of instinctual passion, found within ourselves? Animals like snakes follow God's will not by listening to commands but by obeying their passions, by listening to their natural, God-given instincts and urges. Every time a lioness hunts a gazelle or a grizzly bear plucks a salmon out of an Alaskan river, that animal has followed the voice of God. The snake holds out the possibility that perhaps people should adopt the same approach to their relationship with the Deity: "Even if God said do not eat from the trees of the Garden... [so what]?"

God may have *told* you not to eat from the tree, but do you want to? If so, you are faced with a contradiction. Which divine voice will you listen to – God's *spoken* words, or the voice of God that beats insistently *inside* you – the voice of instinct, passion and desire? Speaking for myself, the snake argues, it is not much of a contest. For an animal, the voice of desire always reigns supreme.

In the act of reaching for the Forbidden Fruit, Adam and Eve succumbed to the snake's argument. As a result, they changed. In eating from the Tree of Desire, Adam and Eve took desire inside themselves and began to identify the core of their selfhood in desire. This increased the centrality, and hence the energy, of the engine burning inside of them, but it also introduced an element of imbalance into their identity. When you are driving your car but are sitting on top of the engine instead of behind the steering wheel, how do you guide the car effectively anymore? This is the question that Cain and all subsequent inhabitants of the post-Tree world are left to grapple with.

From Eden to Cain

At first glance, the story of Cain and Abel, seems a sorry tale of sibling rivalry getting tragically out of hand. But the story is about so much more than sibling rivalry. Cain is contending with a deep passion, a force of dizzying power, that wishes so to speak, to bond with him and fill him with its life-affirming power. Cain, for his part, must realize that as benevolent and tantalizing as this force is, he is not the same as it; he is distinct from it. He must affirm his identity outside of it, and somehow, he must rule over it. He must direct its power.

What is the name of that passion?

Did you ever wonder why Adam and Eve, in the wake of eating from the Tree of Knowledge, were – of all things – fearful of their nakedness? If they sensed that the desires and passion within themselves were stronger than before, that these were now forces to be feared, why was it specifically their *nakedness*, their new consciousness of sexuality that they feared? There are other passions in the world. Why is sexuality singled out?

The answer, I think, is that the Tree of Knowledge was not just about passion in general. It was about *a particular kind of passion*:

The snake argued to Eve: "God ate from this tree and created the world. He doesn't want you to eat from it, for if you do, you will be empowered to create worlds, too. Everyone knows that a craftsman hates his competitors..." (Midrash Rabbah on Genesis, 19:4)

According to the Midrash, the Tree of Knowledge was about the mysterious and sublime drive *to create*.

In the realm of human biology, creativity expresses itself in sexuality. Hence, immediately after eating from the tree, Adam and Eve fear their nakedness. They feel dwarfed by this force called sexuality. But creativity expresses itself in other realms, too. One of those realms is agriculture. In agriculture, creativity expresses itself as the desire to plant.

Sexuality and Planting

Cain, the first living product of the miracle we call human sexuality – the child of a mother who exclaims in ecstasy that she has acquired a man with God – chooses to become a farmer. We argued earlier that this is not a coincidence. Cain devotes his life to creation with land, just as his mother has created with her womb.

The drive to create – or even better, the drive to create in partnership with God – may be the deepest passion we human beings can know. This passion is so deep and sublime that it is quite nearly godly. As our friend the snake once said, if you eat from the tree, "you shall be as gods, knowing good and evil" (Genesis 3:4).

But ironically, this same passion can also be the source of great evil. Indeed, as we explained previously, "Evil Inclination" is only an approximate translation. The original Hebrew words are *yetzer hara*, the term "yetzer" coming from "yotzer," which means "to create." Rendered literally, the Evil Inclination, at bottom, seems to be nothing more than the drive to create gone awry.

What the Almighty was telling Cain, I think, is that even a passion as holy as the drive to join with God in acts of creation must still be channeled. As ironic as it sounds, this apparently spiritual drive is potentially destructive. It can drive a wedge between humans and the source of all creativity, God Himself. Whether creativity becomes holy or destructive mostly depends on who is doing the driving: the engine or the steering wheel.

What, precisely, does holy creativity look like, and how do you tell the difference between it and its fraternal twin, destructive creativity? These are the questions that God's speech puts before us, front and center. And it is to these questions that we shall return in the coming pages.

℘ Chapter Thirteen
Of Roses and Triangles

"Its teshukah is for you, yet you can rule over it…"

If the "yetzer" of Cain is the drive to create, the passion to plant crops and create in partnership with God, what would it mean for Cain to rule over this? The answer will take us back to the story of Thomas Edison and the glassblower.

The glassblower was fired with the passion to create in partnership with Edison. The crucial question for him was: How would this affect his relationship with Edison? Would it destroy that relationship or enhance it? It would all depend on whether the glassblower could rule over his passion, or whether his passion would rule over him.

If the glassblower is consumed by his desire to create, if he is held in its thrall – well, that alone is not sinful, but "sin lies crouching at the door," as it were. The glassblower may find himself viewing Edison merely as a tool to realize his own creative ambitions. His goal in giving a gift to Edison would thus be little more than bribery, a bald-faced attempt to ensure that the inventor does not get himself another glassblower.

And so it might be with Cain. When the drive to join God

in the act of creation is left undirected, it can slowly become an obsession, a powerful, gnawing end in itself. When this happens, anything can be sacrificed on its altar – even, ironically, Cain's relationship with God Himself. If I see God as a necessary instrument to make my creativity flourish, to let my crops grow, I may relentlessly try to "buy Him off." As I reach brazenly for the keys to the Heavenly Cookie Jar, I'll give God plenty of gifts, but gifts of a curiously average quality. I offer to my Heavenly Partner only what is necessary to ensure his continued co-operation in our mutual endeavor.

There is, however, an alternative. Cain, like the glassblower, has a choice to make. Rather than be *controlled* by the monumental passion to create with God, he can *rule over* it. He can direct the power of this force. He can direct it toward the heroic stance we call gratitude.

If Cain can but steer his passion, it will become an engine for something profoundly positive. The offering that Cain gives will not be about bribery, but about overwhelming gratitude. It will not be a crass attempt to ensure that the keys to the Heavenly Cookie Jar always remain comfortably within reach. It will be something infinitely more valuable – a humble expression of appreciation for letting me share in the secret of creation with my Creator, the Creator of All.

Roses for Dad and Mom

The difference between the two stances, and between the impact each has on the relationship between creature and Creator, could not be more significant.

We can see this when we consider our own relationships with those we create, namely, our children. Here's a scenario: Sam and his fiancée have just arrived at his parents' home for their first visit since Sam graduated from medical school. Mom and Dad are flattered to notice that the couple has brought them flowers. But what do the flowers mean? Mom and Dad have spent a good deal of toil and treasure to put Sam through medical school. If the flowers are expressions of gratitude, if they signify their child's deeply felt recognition of the great gift they have given to him – well, there is nothing that warms a parent's heart more than this. Such a gift contributes powerfully to the quality of the relationship between parent and child.

But what if the roses are *not* about gratitude? Sam and his new bride will look to his parents for considerable help in the future as they struggle through years of internship and residency. What if the flowers are a calculated attempt to keep Mom and Dad happy? What if Sam and his bride are giving a perfunctory, average gift that will serve nicely, they hope, as an insurance policy to ensure Dad and Mom's continued support?

There is no greater heartbreak than receiving a gift like this. One suspects it is better to give nothing at all. A gift that is a mere insurance policy demeans the relationship between parent and child. It cheapens the natural love of a creator for his offspring by turning that love into a mere commodity to be hoarded, to be squirreled away for a rainy day. Worse, it turns the creator into a mere tool of the child's creativity, a creativity that ultimately becomes self-centered and self-serving. The creator becomes nothing but a pawn in a great chess game that revolves insidiously around the ever-expanding ambitions of the child.

Cain brings the quintessential "average" gift to his Creator, and the Almighty, the Great Parent in the Sky, takes Cain aside to have a little talk with him about all this:

Why are you angry and why has your face fallen? He asks Cain. Your anger and depression are out of place, for the ball is entirely in your court: *If you do well,* if you guide your powerful desire to create along with Me, *you can lift up [your face].* A gift that expresses gratitude will always be accepted by your Creator, and you can look yourself in the eye in the mirror after giving it. *But if you do not do well,* if you fail to steer your passion, if you adopt a position of neutrality, then *sin lies crouching at the door.*

You risk sacrificing our very relationship on the altar of blind creativity. *The teshukah of your passion is for you, yet you can rule over it*; you can transform its raw power into gratitude, into something that enhances rather than destroys our relationship.

Cain does not listen. He persists in his belief that the source of his problems lies outside of himself, that he has been victimized by someone else, anyone else. He cannot kill God for failing to accept his gift – the Almighty is impervious to arrows and spears – so he does the next best thing. He lashes out in a different direction, killing Abel, the brother whose offering found favor with his Maker.

Cain's rage, like the surging creativity inside him, is blind. His act of murder does not appear premeditated; it seems spontaneous.* Indeed, the Sages tell us that Cain killed inadvertently. He did not know that his violence would destroy Abel, as the ultimate fruits of physical brutality were, at the time, a great unknown.† No one had ever been killed before. Tragically, Cain is perhaps

---

* The Torah states that before Cain killed Abel, both brothers were in the field, and the beginning of a conversation ensued between them. But it was only the *beginning* of a conversation. Most translations will render the action leading up to murder in something like the following terms: "Cain spoke to Abel, and it happened, when they were both in the field, [that] Cain came upon Abel and killed him." The problem, though, is that the Hebrew term for Cain's speaking to Abel is not *vayedaber* but *vayomer*, which means that the text does not really translate as "Cain *spoke* to Abel" but "Cain *said* to Abel". This, however, creates a non-sequitur: If I tell you that x spoke to y, I don't need to tell you what was said between them, but if I tell you that x *said* to y, I *do* have to tell you what was said, or else the sentence is incomplete. The sense of the verse, therefore, is of an interrupted conversation, that Cain started saying something to Abel, and, by rights, we should hear what it is – but before actually getting to it, Cain interrupted what he was saying and killed Abel instead. The murder was an impulsive, violent end to something that perhaps could have been resolved through mere words.

† According to one Midrash (Midrash Rabbah, Deuteronomy 2:26), this explains why Cain's punishment was exile. Later passages in the Torah set forth that a murderer who deliberately kills is subject to capital punishment, but one who kills inadvertently, or without full knowledge of what he is doing, is

being truthful when he tells God that he simply does not know where Abel is anymore. But none of that matters; what is done is done and cannot be taken back. Abel's blood cries out from the ground. Creativity has caught up with Cain. The beast is no longer crouching at the door. It has sprung, devouring both killer and victim within its jaws.

The Core of the Triangle

At long last, we are in a position to see the global picture, the composite portrait painted for us in these first two human dramas in the Book of Genesis, the sagas of the Forbidden Fruit and the World's First Murder. As we have seen, both stories revolve around the proper role of creativity in the psyche of humankind. Failure in one story brought death into the world in theory, while failure in the other brought death into the world in practice. Failure in each story brought exile, difficulty in farming, and hiding from God.

We have seen that the story of Adam and Eve is closely connected to the story of Cain and Abel. The latter doesn't just *happen* to come after the former; it really is its sequel, conceptually and thematically. A process starts in the first story, and that process takes another step in the second story. And each of these steps is accompanied by three, interrelated consequences: exile, difficulty in farming, and hiding from God.

As we draw our meditation on these stories to a close, we may wonder: "Why?" Why, in fact, does failure to wield passion properly, failure to harness properly the fiery will to create – why does this kind of failure lead to these particular consequences?

We began to ponder this question in Part One, but I think we are now in a position to understand it more deeply. Before you turn the page and begin the final portions of this book, I'd like you to stop and think about these three things: exile, difficulty in

instead exiled from his land (Numbers 35:22–25). Cain's exile, according to the Midrash, was the prototype for that law.

farming, and hiding from God. Ask yourself: How, if at all, are these things related to one another? What is the core of this three-sided triangle? Is there a common drum-beat to which they all step? I think that there is.

૭ Chapter Fourteen

There's No Place Like Home

Exile; difficulty in farming; hiding from God – is there a common theme? We can begin by doing a little consolidating. As we observed earlier, the Torah treats exile and difficulty farming as dual expressions of a larger idea – the advent of a certain distance between man and the land:

> …And now, cursed are you from the land that opened its maw to take your brother's blood from your hands. When you work the land, it will no longer give its strength to you; a wanderer shall you be in the land…" (Genesis 4:11–12)

We can think of these words as forming a kind of triangle. The fact that Cain is cursed from the earth – distanced from the land – is the top of the triangle, the "topic-sentence," as it were. The two points at the base of the triangle then clarify what this "distance from the land" means in real life: it means that you will experience difficulty in farming and exile. These two things express a kind of alienation Cain will feel with respect to the land.

Cursed from the Land

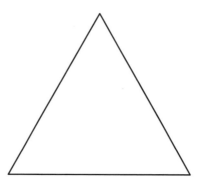

Difficulty in Farming   Exile from the Land

We can now go back and simplify our inquiry. Having identified the unifying theme in "difficulty in farming" and "exile," we are now looking for common denominators between two elements rather than three. We now want to know: what do "distance from the earth" and "hiding from God" have in common?*

Well, the ideas of "hiding" and "distance" are certainly similar. When one hides from someone else, one is avoiding contact with them, creating distance. Now let's ask: what, if anything, do "earth" and "God" have in common?

At first glance, you might answer that "earth" and "God" could not be more different. One is the Master of the Universe; the other, a part of that universe. One is the most powerful Being in existence; the other, merely an inanimate object.

But there *is* a similarity. We get a clue to that connection in the anguish Cain feels at the prospect of alienation from both God and land: "'My sin is greater than I can bear. Here, you have

---

* This perspective is confirmed by a later verse in which Cain summarizes his punishments using the following language: "My sin is greater than I can bear. Here you have cast me away from the face of the earth and from the face of God I will hide." In Cain's view, his suffering is about two things: distance from land and distance from God.

cast me away from the face of the land, and from Your face I will hide…'" (Genesis 4:13).

We explained previously that the verb for "cast away" is the same as the Hebrew word for divorce (*gerashti*). Something intensely personal is occurring here: the land, like God, is an important being in Cain's life, yet Cain is banished from beholding the "face" of either:

> "…you have cast me away *from the face* of the land, and *from Your face* I will hide… "

Why is all this so personal?

Let Us Make Man

Some earlier verses will help our understanding. Back in the beginning of Genesis, when humanity is first created, the Almighty uses a curious turn of phrase. "Let us make man," He declares (Genesis 1:26). Over the ages, biblical commentators have struggled to understand the use of the plural here. Who was God talking to when He said "us"?

The great commentator Rashi (eleventh-century France) suggests that perhaps God was speaking to the angels; but Nachmanides (thirteenth century, Spain) has a particularly fascinating interpretation. He writes the following:

> It was only on the first day of creation that God created something from nothing. From then on, He fashioned everything from the elements He had brought into being on the first day. For example, He empowered water to give rise to living things, as it is stated "let the water swarm…," and He allowed animal life to emerge from the land, as the verse states: "Let the land bring forth living things" (Genesis 1:23). When He created man, though, the Lord said: "Let *us* make man…" In so doing, the Almighty was speaking to the earth – the last "being" to bring forth life [see the immediately preceding

verse about earth "bringing forth" the animals]. In effect, He was saying: "You and I together will make man. You will contribute the elements for the body, as you did for the animals, and I will contribute the soul," as it is written: "and He breathed into his nostrils the breath of life..." (Nachmanides to Genesis 1:26)

The implications of Nachmanides' words are astounding, and not just for the way he anticipates the direction of modern biology, seven centuries before Pasteur, Darwin and Mendel were even a gleam in history's eye. Nachmanides is suggesting here a key to the mysterious connection between humanity and land. People will fight and die for land and will form intense emotional bonds to the ground they call home. Why? Because, at the end of the day, land is not merely a "thing." Along with God, it is the source from which we all come. And because of that, it will always matter personally to us.

A creature always wants a relationship with its Creator. We long to live in harmony with our parents, for as Dorothy famously said, "There's no place like home." On some level, it is to both land and God that humanity longs to return – a dream that, ironically, is perhaps fully realized only in death:

Dust you are, and to the dust you shall return. (Genesis 3:18)

The dust [that comprises the body] shall go back to the land, as it once was; and the spirit will return to the Lord who had imparted it... (Ecclesiastes 12:7).

Cain, God, and Mother Earth

It is no coincidence that we call land "Mother Earth," for she provides humanity with the essential gifts of femininity: nourishment and a safe place to be, a place to call home.

A mother provides a safe environment for her family. This is true not only physically but also emotionally. At its best, a home is a place where children need not fear the caprice and unpredictability of the outside world. Likewise, a mother provides nourishment to her family, not only physically but also emotionally. She provides not just food but love, nurturing her offspring and helping them grow into stable, happy human beings.

A woman gives these twin gifts, nourishment and a place to be, not only to her fully developed family but to her *developing* family as well. She offers them from the very beginning, through the organ that is the embodiment of femininity, the womb. What does a womb provide the fetus ensconced within it? It provides total nourishment as well as a perfectly calibrated "safe place to be," an environment completely insulated from the shocks of the outside world.

Mother Earth provides these gifts to her children, too. She provides us with a place to be, a home where we can live, and she also provides us with nourishment through the agricultural bounty of her fertile soil.

In the wake of Abel's murder, Cain finds himself distanced from both these aspects of the land, and he also finds himself hiding from God. Having failed to give his all to his own Creator, he becomes aware that Mother Earth will no longer give her all to him: "When you work the earth, it will no longer give its strength to you..." (Genesis 4:11). Instinctively, Cain knows exactly what this means. It is a punishment greater than he can bear, because now he has been "cast away" from the "faces" of both Mother Earth and the Almighty, becoming painfully out of touch with those who created him.

At long last, we can go back and plot the continuum of these narratives, the sagas of the Tree of Knowledge and then Cain and Abel, and we can see how they form, almost seamlessly, a single story.

From Forbidden Fruit to Murder

When Adam and Eve ate from the Tree of Knowledge, they identified themselves with their creative will, energized it, and began

179

to see life through the lens of this will. In so doing, they became "godly," after a fashion. God, the ultimate Creator, sees things through the lens of His own Creativity. Things that are in line with God's desire are "good"; things that aren't are "evil."

"And you shall be as gods, knowing good and evil..."

But the humans who ate from the tree were only half-godly. They were passionate, driven, like God, to create and foster new life. But, unlike God, their ability to properly steer this newly fired sense of creativity remained limited and out of proportion with its power.

God's creativity is inherently disciplined. The Creator of All understands that the world needs not just life, but death at the appropriate time as well. When a baby develops in the womb, its hands begin as a kind of formless paddle. Fingers are formed only because skin cells between each of the digits die and fall away, sculpting what we call a hand in the inky blackness of the womb. Death is painful and sad, but necessary. A disciplined Creator works with death as well as life, sculpting with exquisite care everything from galaxies to ecosystems to babies.*

As a consequence of eating from the tree, humanity is powerfully creative, but the question is: can we also be disciplined? The uncertain answer to this question has many consequences.

---

* In Jewish tradition, God is closely associated with the concept of "truth" (e.g., "the seal of the Almighty is truth," Babylonian Talmud, *Shabbat* 55a). In Hebrew, the word "truth" is spelled *aleph, mem*, tav. Its very structure suggests the idea of balance between life and death. How so? Aleph is the first letter of the alphabet; mem the middle letter of the alphabet; and tav is the last. The first and middle letters of the word spell "em" (mother); the middle and last letters spell "met" (death). The seal of God is truth – disciplined creativity. "Emet" suggests the exquisite balance between motherhood, with its intense drive to foster life, and death, which imposes discipline and makes something meaningful out of raw life.

Adam and Eve immediately become fearful of their nakedness, suddenly aware that the raw power of sexuality could crush them. Moreover, humanity – possessor of unbridled creativity – is itself distanced from its own creators, namely, God and land. Finally, humanity flounders amidst its own ability to create: in the wake of the Tree of Knowledge, pain in childbirth enters the world for the first time.

The very next story in the Bible, the saga of Cain and Abel, picks up where the previous episode left off. In the aftermath of the Tree of Knowledge, the great question facing humankind is: how, in fact, will we steer the fearsome forces of our own creativity? Cain must ask himself similar questions. Will he be ruled by his passion to create? Will he end up sacrificing his relationship with God on that altar? Or will he rule over his passion and enhance his relationship with God instead?

In failing to meet this challenge; in failing to see that desire is something he *possesses*, not something he *is*; in failing to guide the inherently blind creative will inside him, Cain suffers an intensification of the consequences felt by his parents. He, like Adam, is alienated from his creators, but more permanently so. He intuits that he will not merely hide from God momentarily, but will spend his life in that state of hiding [...*and from your face I will hide*]. Likewise, he suffers a more profound alienation from Mother Earth – a complete inability to find a home on her soil and utter frustration in reaping the nourishment she can provide.

From Cain's World to Our World

Cain fails. But his story is not over.

"Its desire is unto you, but you can rule over it..."

Although Cain did not listen to what God had to tell him, the words of that speech were not wasted. Cain's predicament is timeless, and the struggle to deal with creativity and somehow channel its force constructively – this challenge is with us as much today as it was then. The words of God's speech to Cain, preserved timelessly in the Torah, speak to *us* as well as to the original recipient of that message. Perhaps, centuries and millennia later, we can find it within ourselves to listen to them.

ℰ Chapter Fifteen
The Death of Cain

How did Cain die? We don't know for sure. The Bible doesn't tell us. But the Sages of the Midrash had something to say about the matter. Working with various clues from the biblical text, they patched together an account of how the man who committed the first murder met his own demise.

The story they tell is bizarre and haunting. At face value, it borders on the absurd. But, as I explained earlier, midrashic stories are not necessarily meant to be interpreted at face value. They often use the language of allegory to point to deeper, underlying currents in a story. For all its improbability, then, the story the Midrash tells about Cain's death may be quite truthful indeed.

Before I reveal the conclusion the Midrash reaches, let's take a look at the biblical clues upon which it is based. As near as I can figure, these are some of the issues that nudged the Sages toward their view of how Cain died.

An Unexplained Fear
The Torah records that after Cain killed Abel, the Lord imposed a number of punishments upon Cain. In response, Cain turned

to God and expressed concern that his own demise would not be long in coming:

> And Cain said to God: "My sin is greater than I can bear... anyone who finds me will kill me." God replied to him: "Therefore, anyone who kills Cain will be avenged sevenfold"; and God placed a mark upon Cain, so that all who found him would not kill him. (Genesis 4:13–15)

We might ask: why exactly does Cain feel so vulnerable? It is true that God has imposed a number of punishments on him, from difficulty in farming to exile, but He has not decreed that Cain deserves to be killed. The Lord has not posted any "Cain: Wanted, Dead or Alive" signs around the local neighborhood. Why, then, is Cain so worried? Moreover, precisely who *are* these other people Cain fears will do him in? The world's aggregate population was pretty tiny at the time. Besides his parents and Mrs. Cain, there weren't too many others around. Whom, really, is Cain afraid of?

Rashi, grandfather of the medieval commentators, is bothered by this question. His answer, which originates in the Midrash, is that the killers Cain feared were not men but animals. That is, in the wake of his act of murder, Cain was worried that a beast might devour him.

Has Rashi solved the problem? Well, perhaps he has explained *who* might kill Cain, but he hasn't explained why. Why would Cain all of a sudden worry that animals would kill him? God didn't command animals to avenge Abel's blood. What's more, if Cain had the means to defend himself adequately against the animal world before he killed Abel, he presumably had these same capabilities afterward, too. Why, all of a sudden, does he become afraid?

The Mystery of "Sevenfold Vengeance"
So Cain's fear of death is one oddity, but it is not the only one. An-

184

other strange thing is God's response to this fear, his promise to Cain that whoever kills him will suffer sevenfold vengeance. Why, for starters, would God want to promise such a thing to Cain? It is one thing to soothe Cain by telling him that he will be protected from would-be-killers; but why extend to Cain, a murderer, the assurance that anyone killing him will be punished seven times more severely than the crime warrants? God didn't extend this courtesy to Abel, the innocent victim of murder. Why extend it to Cain, Abel's killer?

And there's another problem, too. What, exactly, does "sevenfold vengeance" mean? Presumably, the worst thing God could do to a killer of Cain, by way of vengeance, would be to kill that person himself. But that's not *sevenfold* vengeance – that's just plain vanilla vengeance, a simple tit-for-tat. Where does the "seven" part fit in?

A New Theory

A strange verse, tucked away at the end of the story of Cain and Abel, may hold the key to answering these questions. Just after the Torah reveals Cain's punishments, it goes on to give a long list of genealogical tables. We hear all about Cain's descendants; who gave birth to whom and how long they lived. Many may wonder why the Bible felt it necessary to include all this apparently trivial information. But if you stop and actually read these genealogical tables, you will find something curious. The Torah goes into tremendous detail about one particular family, a family appearing at the very end of the chain of descendants. We are told the names and professions of each child; then, strangely enough, the text quotes verbatim a short and cryptic declaration made by the father of these children.

In that speech, the father tells of having killed a man. He also refers to the "sevenfold vengeance" of Cain, as well as the vengeance he expects will be exacted against him, a latter-day killer. And what's more, if we bother to count all the "who-begat-whom's" in between, we will find that this mysterious mention of murder occurs precisely – wouldn't you know it – in the seventh generation removed from Cain.

An interesting possibility begins to unfold. Maybe these verses describe the execution of Cain's mysterious sevenfold vengeance. Maybe the phrase "sevenfold" didn't refer to the *severity* of the vengeance (that someone killing Cain would be killed seven times over) but to the *time at which the vengeance occurs*. Maybe the anticipated vengeance would take place after a sevenfold lapse in generations, and maybe this is precisely what we are reading about at the very end of Cain's genealogical table.

Such a possibility bears further exploration. So let's take a closer look at these strange events that occur seven generations removed from Cain. What, in fact, happened in that anticipated "seventh generation"?

The *Lemech* Connection

Only a few details are unambiguous. We are introduced to a man named Lemech, and we are told that he has two wives and four children, three boys and a girl. We know their names. The three boys are Yaval, Yuval and Tuval-Kayin, and the girl is named Na'ama. Yaval becomes the "father of all shepherds and tent-dwellers." Yuval becomes the "father of harps and cymbals," i.e., the inventor of the first musical instruments. And Tuval-Kayin is the inventor of ironworks, the first to fashion metal weaponry.

The Torah then tells us that one day, Lemech convened his two wives and made a disturbing speech to them:

> Listen to my voice, wives of Lemech, hearken to my words:
> For I have killed a man to my injury, and a child to my wound.
> Yes, sevenfold was the vengeance of Cain; and Lemech, seventy-seven." (Genesis 4:23–24)

Lemech's declaration is difficult to decipher, to say the least. He talks about having killed a man and a child, and refers, strangely, to the promise of his ancestor's sevenfold vengeance. What does he mean to say?

The Sages' Parable

The Sages of the Midrash gathered the various puzzle pieces of Lemech's story and constructed a parable to interpret it. In the ensuing Midrash, we learn how Cain died. Here is what the Midrash says:

> Lemech was a seventh-generation descendant of Cain. He was blind, and he would go out hunting with his son, [Tuval-Kayin]. [His son] would lead him by the hand, and when he would see an animal, he would inform his father, [who would proceed to hunt it]. One day, [Tuval-Kayin] cried out to his father: "I see something like an animal over there." Lemech pulled back on his bow and shot.…The child peered from afar at the dead body…and said to Lemech: "What we killed bears the figure of a man, but it has a horn protruding from its forehead." Lemech then exclaimed in anguish: "Woe unto me! It is my ancestor, Cain!" And he clapped his hands together in grief. In doing so, though, he unintentionally struck Tuval-Kayin and killed him, too. (*Tanchuma* on Genesis, 11)

What a strange story! We hear of a hunt gone awry, with a blind Lemech shooting arrows at the beck and call of his over-eager son, little Tuval-Kayin. We hear of an elderly Cain being mistaken for an animal, walking around with a strange horn protruding from its head. What exactly was Cain doing parading around the forest in a unicorn costume?

This much is clear: according to the Sages, the "man" Lemech killed "to [his] injury" was none other than Cain, and the "child" he struck "to his wound" was his own son, Tuval-Kayin. If we put two and two together, the Midrash seems to take the position that when God talked about "sevenfold vengeance" for Cain, He wasn't talking about punishing Cain's murderer. Instead, God was talking about punishing Cain himself. He was promising that Cain himself would be killed in vengeance for Abel's murder – but that this would occur only after a sevenfold lapse in generations.*

The Advent of the Unicorn

So where *did* Cain get that unicorn costume? Why did he have a horn, of all things, sticking out of his forehead? It is time to revisit, one last time, the story of Adam and Eve in Eden – the story where the cascade leading to Cain and Abel first begins.

To this point, our study has repeatedly emphasized the connections between the Cain and Abel narrative and the story of Adam and Eve in the Garden. A triad of consequences – exile, difficulty in farming, hiding from God – besets humankind after they eat from the Tree, and these same consequences reappear, only more intensely, after Cain kills Abel. The Torah, as we have seen, presents the Cain and Abel episode as a continuation of the story of the Tree of Knowledge. Cain's act of murder was fundamentally similar to Adam and Eve's eating from the tree. It was just another chapter in the same saga.

If we had to boil down that saga to just a single, simple sentence, what would we say that these two, linked stories, are about? We might say they are about what it really means to be a human being and not an animal.

In Eden, humanity was accosted by the primal serpent – an

---

* In elaborating this point, Rashi notes a grammatical oddity in the verse in question and suggests that the phrase "whoever kills Cain/sevenfold he will be avenged" should actually be read as two entirely separate statements, one referring to avenging Cain; the other, to avenging Abel. First, God states "whoever kills Cain..." and the rest of the thought is left unsaid, implying an unspoken threat: "Whoever kills Cain...*well, we won't even talk about what happens to him.*" As for the rest of the phrase, "sevenfold will he be avenged," Rashi suggests that this refers to the way Abel's killer will be avenged. That is, the verse is telling us that Cain will eventually have to pay with his life for killing Abel – but that he has a seven-generation grace period before vengeance occurs.

animal that walked, talked, and apparently was an intelligent being. In fact, the snake was very nearly human, so that the challenge the snake proffers to humanity touches on how we define
ourselves in relation to him – that is, "what makes *us* human and
him a snake?" The snake began his words with: "Even if God said
don't eat from the tree, [so what?]." God may have told you not
to eat of the tree, but those words are belied by your desires. Do
you *want* to eat? If so, God is talking to you through that desire.
He put those instincts inside you, and you obey God by following them.

In making this argument, the snake was faithfully representing the perspective of the animal world. The dividing line between
human and animal, we have argued, lies the nature of one's essential self, and how one perceives God "speaking" to one's self.
An animal experiences its "self" as the sum total of its desires. A
human experiences his or her self as a consciousness that rises
above and beyond desire, which can critically evaluate desire and
decide whether to act upon it. In each case, God addresses the
"essential self" of the being to whom He is talking. God speaks to
an animal through its desire; God speaks to humankind by ad-
dressing our minds.

The snake held out the possibility that perhaps humans
should adopt the same approach as the animal world: "Don't listen to God's commands, listen to the voice of passion and instinct,
God's voice that speaks to you from the inside. Therein resides
the real 'you'." For an animal, the voice of desire always reigns
supreme.

In the act of reaching for the Forbidden Fruit, Adam and Eve
succumbed to the snake's argument. In accepting the argument
that, for humans, too, internal desire could be the final arbiter of
God's Will, humanity identified its core with desire. We lost a little
bit of ourselves and became a little more snake-like.

As a result of that failure, God punished all the relevant parties. The snake's "punishment," though, is particularly interesting.
He was told that henceforth he would eat dust, crawl on his belly,

and that hatred and strife would reign in the relationship between his progeny and the children of Eve. The common denominator in these three punishments is evident: the snake would become more obviously different – a being that crawls rather than walks, a being subsisting on food that humans would never touch, and a being whose presence registers instinctive alarm and enmity in the collective psyche of humanity. The snake would become more obviously animal-like, more clearly removed from the realm of humans. Having failed once to distinguish ourselves from the animal world, humankind no longer will be faced with as subtle and dangerous a temptation.

Still, humanity's struggle to define itself in relation to the animal world continued. The story of Cain and Abel was a subsequent battle in the same war – a war centered on how people are meant to relate to their passions, the creative will surging inside them. Cain became enamored of his own ability to create in partnership with God. He was entranced by the products of that enterprise. In the end, that became his core. He sacrificed everything – his relationship with God and the life of his own brother – on that altar. In killing his brother, he had in effect used Abel's blood as fertilizer for the ground. The life of a brother had become a regrettable but acceptable casualty of Cain's continuing, intoxicating quest to bring forth life from the ground. As it did in Eden, blind desire once again held sway.

In the wake of that basic failure, Cain began to fear that beasts would kill him. Why? Because Cain has lost a further battle in the war over what makes us human and not animals. He has become a little more animal-like in submitting to the blind will of desire. Normally, the animal world possesses an instinctive fear of the human world, a realm set apart from it. But Cain intuits that he can no longer count on that fear. The line separating him from beast has become blurred. In the wake of his act of violence, the beasts might now perceive that Cain really was not all that different from them. The days of comfortable distance from the world of the jungle were now behind him.

Cain pleaded to the Almighty for protection from these new-found threats. And the Lord acceded to that request, giving Cain a mark for protection from anyone seeking to molest him. We wondered earlier why it is "fair" that Cain, a murderer, would merit special protection from death at the hands of others. But that mark, the Midrash is saying, was not a supernatural sign promising heavenly retribution to anyone who harmed Cain, nor was it some artificial device to convince the animals that Cain really was a human to be feared after all. Instead, the sign, as the Midrash tells it, was a simple animal's horn. Having become vulnerable to his new compatriots in the world of the jungle, it is only fair that Cain be given a horn, the same means of defense available to any other beast.

Yet in a savage twist of irony, in the end it is precisely the horn given to Cain for protection that does him in. Little Tuval-Kayin sees Cain's horn and immediately assumes that he has sighted a beast. Upon closer examination, though, the boy isn't so sure. The body of the figure is man-like, and he can't figure out whether their kill had been man or beast. He can't tell, not because he can't see well – that's his father's problem, not his – but because the identity of his prey *really is* uncertain: Cain has crossed into the no-man's land between human and animal. Cain, the person who feared he would be killed by an animal, is killed because a person couldn't tell whether he was, in fact, man or animal.

The Child and the Blind Hunter

The midrashic story is interesting not only for the way it portrays Cain, but for its view of Cain's killer as well. The image of Tuval-Kayin and Lemech, the child and the blind hunter, is a memorable one. To fully understand its significance, I propose we take a quick look at the larger, extended family.

Tuval-Kayin, the child weapon-maker, has two brothers – men by the names of Yuval and Yaval. If you replay the names of these three siblings over in your mind, they should sound vaguely familiar. Yuval, Yaval, and Tuval-Kayin. What do they remind you of?

Well, to tell the truth, if you are used to reading the Bible in English, they may not remind you of much. But if you switch to Hebrew, the resonance in these names is unmistakable. The Hebrew original for the name "Cain" is Kayin, which reappears in the appellation given his descendant, Tuval-Kayin. Likewise, the Hebrew name for "Abel" is Hevel or Haval, which sounds suspiciously similar to the descendant we meet seven generations later, "Yaval."

Kayin and Hevel are brothers; Tuval-Kayin and Yaval are brothers. But the resemblance goes beyond names, too. Just as we are told the professions of Cain and Abel, we are told the professions of Tuval-Kayin and Yaval. And, wouldn't you know it, the professions adopted by these seventh-generation descendants are strikingly similar to the arts practiced by their forebears. Cain/Kayin was the word's first killer, and Tuval-Kayin, his namesake-descendant, makes weaponry. Abel/Haval is the first shepherd in history, and his namesake-descendant in the seventh generation is Yaval, the father of traveling herdsmen.

These connections did not go unnoticed by the Sages of the Midrash. Rashi observes, for example, that Tuval-Kayin's name signifies that "he perfected (*metavel*)* the arts of Kayin" (Rashi to Genesis 4:22). Cain killed without benefit of tools; Tuval-Kayin came along and, by forging weaponry, gave the art of killing a technological boost. Yaval, the seventh-generation heir to Haval/Abel, arguably did likewise. He perfected the art of Abel. Abel, the ancestor, grazed his flocks, but Yaval pushed the envelope further. As Rashi put it, he – the "father of herdsmen" – constantly moved his tents, transporting flocks from pasture to pasture, to ensure a virtually never-ending supply of grassland (see Rashi to 4:20).†

---

* In Hebrew, "*metavel*" ("one who perfects") is the verb form of the name "Tuval."

† The middle brother, Yuval, seemingly has no analogue in the Cain and Abel saga, in which there were only two brothers. We might speculate, though, that his name – Yuval – seems to be a cross between *Tuval*-Kayin and *Yaval*. Indeed, his craft, the making of musical instruments, might be seen as a cross between

These great leaps forward all take place in the seventh generation after Cain and Abel. Seven, in the Torah, is a number laden
with symbolic import. It often signifies completion – bringing
a process to its culmination. God completed Creation in seven
days, bringing the Universe to its finished state of being. After
forty-nine years – seven times seven – the Jubilee year (*Yovel*) is
celebrated, when "freedom is proclaimed throughout the land"
and everything attains a new homeostasis, a new balance. Debts
are forgiven and slaves are released from servitude. At the end
of seven generations, the lines of Cain and Abel reach their fruition, too.

In the case of Cain, that destiny bears ominous overtones.
His seventh-generation descendant, Tuval-Kayin, the metal-
worker, takes the art of killing to new and more powerful levels, making weapons that would have been unimaginable to Cain
himself, the ancestor of it all. But such is the way of things. We
don't always have control over the forces we set in motion.

Cain is powerless to stem the lethal forces he has begun to
unleash, forces that culminate in the personage of Tuval-Kayin.
But ironically, Tuval-Kayin and Lemech – the new killers – are, in
their own ways, just as powerless in the face of these forces.

When you get right down to it, the partnership of Tuval-
Kayin and Lemech has to be the craziest hunting duo one could
possibly imagine. Tuval-Kayin spots a leopard at a hundred paces
and calls out the coordinates to his father. Lemech, who can't see
a blasted thing, wheels around sixty degrees to his left, takes a
moment to calculate range and trajectory, then lets his arrows fly.
The image of a child weapon-maker leading his blind father on
hunting expeditions is comedic, but chilling. Neither the father
nor the child is in control. Neither is quite aware of the awesome
power they so irresponsibly wield. Both are powerful engines – but
nothing of consequence guides either of them.

the pastoral profession of shepherding and the technological innovations of
metallurgy and practical tool-making.

Three Blind Men

A quick survey of blind men in the Bible turns up an interesting pattern. Lemech, according to the Sages, was blind. Isaac, toward the end of his life, suffered from failing eyesight. And so did Eli, the high priest mentioned at the beginning of I Samuel. Sensing a commonality here, the Sages of the Midrash commented: "Anyone who raises a wicked son or trains a wicked disciple is destined eventually to lose his eyesight" (Midrash Rabbah on Genesis, 65:9).

The Sages were not doctors, and the observation they made was not necessarily medical in nature, but spiritual. Why would a father who raises wicked children eventually become blind? Perhaps the Sages were not talking about the physical inability to see, but an emotional blindness – a deep-seated *unwillingness* to see. Isaac can't bring himself to face the true nature of Esau, and Eli can't bear to face the sins his sons commit. These otherwise prescient fathers are blind to what is obvious to all others around them. When reality is too cruel to see, the best among us can easily make themselves blind to its horror.

In the view of the Midrash, Lemech, like Isaac and Eli, is blind. It is not so much that his son is evil – after all, Tuval-Kayin is only a child – but the dangers of his craft are entirely lost on the oblivious father. There is a kid out there making sawed-off shotguns, and instead of restraining him, Lemech invites little Tuval out for hunting parties. Lemech can easily rationalize the deadly arts of his son – after all, it is not guns that kill people, but people that kill people – and if all my boy does is make the swords that others use… well, that's a good, clean living, isn't it? The mandate of parents is to guide their children, but in this case it is little Tuval-Kayin who is the leader, guiding – with devastating inaccuracy – the arrows of his blind father.

The seventh generation is the apogee, and in it the generations of Cain are slowly spinning out of control. Tuval-Kayin really is, "Cain Perfected." Cain failed to rule over the raging passions that beset his soul, and Lemech has failed to rule over the raging power of his young son's killing machines. Seven generations from Cain, nothing has changed; it is just the stakes that have gotten higher. The legacy of the Forbidden Fruit is alive and well. Humanity is becoming ever more snake-like, as raw power, left to its own devices, consistently overwhelms its bearer.

The Second Lemech and the Wife of Noah

The children of Lemech are the last descendants of Cain that the world will ever know. The great Flood – the ultimate destruction of humanity – is right around the corner. A glimmer of hope, though, beckons to humanity.

Right after the Torah finishes telling us of Cain's seven generations of descendants – indeed, immediately after Lemech's disastrous pronouncement of "seventy-seven-fold vengeance" – the Torah relates something fascinating. We hear of a second chain of generations, beginning with the birth of a child named Shet (Genesis 4:25). Shet was a third son born to Eve, a son born after Cain killed Abel, and the text tells us that Shet, in Eve's mind, constituted a replacement of sorts for her murdered son, Abel (Genesis 4:25). Interestingly, the list of Shet's descendants is introduced with the words: *"These are the generations of Adam"* – as if to say that these are the *real* generations of Adam. And they are. After all, Abel was murdered and had no children. Cain's children are wiped out after seven generations in the great flood. It is really only this last child, Shet, who allows the generations of Adam to continue in perpetuity. For Noah – the saving remnant of humanity – is a descendant of Shet.

Strangely, as you begin to go through them, the descendants of Shet sound a lot like the descendants of Cain. For example, Cain has a descendant named Metushael, and Shet has a descendant named Metushelech. Cain has a child by the name of Chanoch, and Shet has a descendant by the same name. Curiously, Shet's immediate offspring is a child named "Enosh," a word which (like Adam) has come to mean "man", and the child of Enosh is Keinan, which seems a variation on Kayin/Cain. It is as if Shet's own line of heirs contains a mirror both of Adam himself and of Adam's son, Cain.

Well, it can't come as too much of a surprise that a seventh-generation descendant of Enosh – this second Adam – is a child named… you guessed it Lemech….* In case you missed the point, this second Lemech just happens to live to the ripe old age of – seven hundred and seventy-seven years. So, when all is said and done, at seven generations, each line – the line of Adam I and Adam II (Enosh) – come to their apex; both produce a Lemech. But whereas the first Lemech gives birth to Tuval-Kayin, a son who becomes a partner in the destruction of life, the second Lemech gives birth to a son who will allow for the perpetuation of life. The child of Lemech II is a man by the name of Noah.

While the three sons of Lemech I die in a flood, the child of Lemech II builds an ark. And yet, while the children of Lemech I perish in that flood, the legacy of Lemech I is not erased entirely. One of his children, according to the Sages, survives. According to the Midrash, his daughter Na'amah (the sister of Tuval-Kayin) becomes the wife of Noah (Midrash Rabbah on Genesis 23:3).

So a daughter of Lemech I survives by marrying the son of Lemech II. In that union, humanity comes full circle. The doomed line of Cain merges with a spark of life from Shet, the man who, according to Eve, was a replacement for Abel. At long last, the legacies of Cain and "replacement Abel" have come together, as a father from one line and a mother from the other unite in the ark to perpetuate humanity anew.

When we look back on Cain and his legacy, it is easy to disregard him, to feel that humanity is better off without having to deal with the wickedness he manifests. But evidently, Abel – or his replacement – is not enough of a foundation upon which to build a new world. For all the danger he brings to the table, Cain

---

* This Lemech, like the first one, is born seven generations after Enosh and Adam, respectively. Moreover, this second Lemech lives for a total of 777 years. The connections between Lemech and the theme of seven are quite intense.

is a necessary partner. Somehow, humanity needs the energies of both Cain and Abel – ground, coupled with nothingness; possession, bound together with breath – to move on, to build itself in perpetuity. And so it is that – in the personhood of Noah and Na'amah – under the live-saving roof of an ark, a fragmented humanity finally gains a semblance of unity, just as the storm-clouds of apocalypse gather on the horizon.

৾ About the Author

Rabbi David Fohrman is resident scholar at the Hoffberger Foundation for Torah Studies and an adjunct professor at the Johns Hopkins University where he teaches Biblical Themes. He also teaches at Yeshivat Sha'alvim and Yeshiva University's Gruss Kollel in Jerusalem.

Rabbi Fohrman was educated at Ner Israel Rabbinical College, as well as the Johns Hopkins University. He now lives in Nof Ayalon, Israel, with his wife and children.

He has served for seven years as a writer and editor for ArtScroll's Schottenstein Edition of the Talmud, lectures widely throughout the United States, and teaches classes over the Internet using an innovative interactive format. Recent classes include: "The Phantom Akeidah," "A Brief History of the World from Adam to Abraham," and "Shattered Tablets and a Calf of Gold."

Rabbi Fohrman's Internet classes can be found at www.jewishtextstudy.org. In addition, a wide variety of his talks are available in audio form through www.jewishexplorations.com.